THE INDIA STORY

WHERE TRADITION MEETS TRANSFORMATION

MANASI MEHTA

Made with ♥ on the Notion Press Platform
www.notionpress.com

To my parents,

For being my first teachers,
This book is a testament to the lessons you've instilled in
me—
to honor my roots while reaching for the skies.

Contents

Author's Note

This book comes from my deep love for India and its rich traditions. As a writer, I feel blessed to share my connection with the essence of this beautiful country. India, with its long history, culture, and wisdom, has always inspired me. This is my first book, and it is a tribute to the traditions that have shaped us and continue to guide us today.

Through these pages, I hope to celebrate the strength and beauty of India's heritage. It is with great respect that I share this work with you, as my small contribution to the story of our amazing nation.

Thank you for joining me on this journey.

— Manasi Mehta

Preface

India is a land where old traditions and modern ideas come together beautifully. It is a country where people move forward with progress while staying connected to their roots. This book, "The India Story – Where Tradition Meets Transformation," is my effort to celebrate this unique balance.

As someone deeply connected to Indian culture and curious about the world, I've often wondered how Indians manage to be modern while holding onto their traditions. I've realized this isn't a conflict but a strength. Our traditions give us the foundation to grow, adapt, and succeed in the modern world.

This book explores how Indian traditions, from the teachings of the Vedas to the practices of yoga and Ayurveda, continue to guide us even today. It also looks at how these traditions help shape modern ideas and inspire progress. I want to show how being rooted in culture doesn't hold us back—it helps us see further and achieve more.

Writing this book has been a journey of learning and reflection. It has made me appreciate the depth of our culture and how it can help us lead better, more balanced lives. I hope this book will encourage readers to see the value of our traditions and how they can guide us towards a brighter future.

To my parents, who taught me the importance of staying rooted, and to my readers, who I hope will find their own inspiration in these pages—this book is for you.

— *Manasi Mehta*

Acknowledgements

This book would not have been possible without the love and support of many people in my life.

To my parents, for your guidance, encouragement, and the values you've taught me. You have been my greatest inspiration and strength.

To my teachers and mentors, your lessons have shaped my understanding of our culture and its importance.

To my friends and family, for your constant support and motivation during this journey. Your belief in me kept me going.

And to my readers, for joining me in exploring the balance between tradition and modernity. I hope this book inspires you as much as writing it inspired me.

I am deeply grateful to all of you.

THE DUALITY OF TRADITION AND MODERNITY

CHAPTER ONE

THE NEED FOR THIS BOOK

India, a land of rich cultural heritage, spiritual wisdom, and diversity, has always been at the crossroads of tradition and modernity. The world often perceives these two forces as conflicting; modernity is often seen as the antithesis of tradition, and vice versa. In India's case, however, these two forces do not compete. Instead, they coexist and, in many ways, complement each other. As the country marches forward into a new era of rapid development, globalization, and technological advancement, it becomes increasingly vital to understand how India is managing this delicate balance between honoring its age-old traditions and embracing the possibilities of the future.

This book seeks to address the crucial need for recognizing the harmonious coexistence of tradition and modernity in India. It challenges the binary perspective of tradition versus modernity and instead explores how the two can work together to shape a progressive, vibrant nation. The need for such a book arises from multiple factors, ranging from global misconceptions about Indian culture to the internal struggle of Indian society to adapt to rapid changes while staying grounded in its roots.

Breaking Stereotypes about Indian Traditions

One of the major reasons for writing this book is the pervasive global misconception about Indian traditions. While many Western nations celebrate innovation and advancement as the ultimate mark of progress, they often view traditions as outdated, restrictive, or regressive. Indian traditions are often misunderstood or oversimplified, leading to a skewed perception of India's identity in the global context. Whether it's the rituals, festivals, or practices that have been passed down through generations, tradition is often portrayed as something that must be abandoned in the pursuit of a "modern" lifestyle.

This book aims to correct this misconception by offering a more nuanced and balanced view. By exploring the deep wisdom embedded in India's traditions, the book will highlight how these age-old practices are not only still relevant but also provide essential solutions to modern challenges. For instance, sustainable living, eco-friendly practices, and mental well-being—core aspects of India's ancient traditions—are rapidly gaining attention in contemporary global discourse. The need for this book is urgent, as it seeks to offer the world a fresh perspective on the intersection of the old and new, demonstrating that traditions can be a source of strength and guidance in today's fast-paced world.

Understanding Modernity in the Indian Context

India is a nation on the rise, both economically and politically. It is home to one of the fastest-growing economies in the world, and yet, it is often confronted with the challenge of how to modernize while preserving its cultural identity. The rapid urbanization and technological advancements have brought about significant changes in Indian society. However, these changes often come with tensions—tensions between the old and the new, the rural and the urban, and tradition versus modernity.

In this context, the book will explore what it truly means to be "modern" in India. It is not enough to simply adopt the latest technological gadgets, consumer goods, or global trends to be considered modern. True modernity, as this book will argue, lies in the ability to innovate and adapt while maintaining a strong connection to one's roots. For India, modernity should not be a Western import or a one-size-fits-all solution. Rather, it should be a unique and tailored response to the country's specific challenges and opportunities, built on the solid foundation of its traditions.

A Guide to Navigating the Complexities of Change

As India enters the global stage, it faces challenges that are unique to its socio-cultural context. The rapid pace of globalization, the migration of people, and the shift toward a more consumer-driven economy have brought with them a set of complexities that the country must navigate. In the midst of this transition, India faces a critical question: How can it retain its unique cultural identity while embracing the benefits of global integration? The need for this book arises from the desire to find a roadmap for this journey.

The book will serve as a guide for individuals and communities trying to navigate these complexities. By discussing the role of education, social media, youth engagement, and policy-making in shaping India's future, the book will provide a roadmap to harmonize tradition and modernity. The core message will focus on how individuals, organizations, and institutions can make the most of the changes happening around them, while staying true to the values and principles that have long been the bedrock of Indian society. Whether it is the professional world, the arts, or social activism, the key lies in balancing progress with purpose—something that India's traditions have always championed.

Addressing Internal Struggles: Balancing Tradition with Progress

While the outside world grapples with its own misconceptions of India's traditions, India itself is undergoing a quiet internal struggle. On the one hand, there is a desire for modernization—be it in the form of economic development, technological innovation, or global influence. On the other hand, there is a deep cultural attachment to practices that have been passed down through generations. For many Indians, there is a concern that the rush towards modernization might lead to the erosion of their cultural identity. The younger generation, especially, is caught between the allure of global trends and the pressure to conform to traditional expectations.

The need for this book is particularly urgent in the context of the younger generation's engagement with tradition. This book will provide insights into how young Indians can embrace modernity while still staying connected to their cultural heritage. It will provide practical suggestions for how traditional wisdom can be integrated into daily life in meaningful ways, whether through family practices, professional ethics, or social responsibility.

The Role of Indian Traditions in Solving Global Problems

Another vital reason for the existence of this book is the global recognition of the value of Indian traditions in solving some of the world's most pressing challenges. Issues like climate change, mental health, and social inequality require not just technological solutions but also a deep cultural shift. Indian philosophies such as *ahimsa* (non-violence), *dharma* (righteous duty), and *seva* (selfless service) offer valuable frameworks for addressing these issues.

The book will discuss how India's ancient traditions provide not just spiritual guidance but also practical solutions for sustainable living, conflict resolution, and community welfare. By examining case studies from across the world, where Indian traditions have been successfully integrated into global practices, the book will make a compelling case for why the world needs to look beyond Western ideologies and consider India's unique contributions to modern global issues.

A Call for a New Perspective on India's Role in the World

In an increasingly interconnected world, India's role on the global stage is becoming more significant. The book will provide a fresh perspective on India's leadership, based on its ability to harmonize tradition with modernity. This perspective is crucial for global peace, prosperity, and sustainable development. In a world divided by political, economic, and cultural lines, India's example of blending heritage with innovation could serve as a model for others.

In conclusion, this book addresses the pressing need to rethink how we understand tradition and modernity, not just in India but across the globe. By recognizing the inherent strength of Indian traditions and the transformative power of modernity, we can foster a future where progress does not come at the expense of culture but instead is built upon it. This book invites readers to explore the many facets of India's unique journey and to appreciate the profound wisdom that lies at the intersection of its ancient past and its modern future.

CHAPTER TWO

Exploring the Global Misconceptions

India, a nation of contrasts and complexities, has long been a subject of fascination, admiration, and misunderstanding. While the country has made remarkable strides in various fields like technology, economics, and global diplomacy, a host of global misconceptions still persist. These misunderstandings about India often stem from stereotypes, oversimplifications, and a lack of genuine awareness about the true diversity and dynamism of Indian society. From its ancient roots to its modern-day achievements, India is a land of paradoxes, where ancient traditions coexist with cutting-edge innovation. However, these complexities are often lost in the global narrative.

The most enduring misconception about India is that the country is trapped in the past, unable or unwilling to embrace modernity. This narrative often portrays India as a place where traditions hold the country back from moving forward, a place where people are rigidly attached to customs that impede progress. Such portrayals are rooted in a narrow and incomplete understanding of Indian society. While India has a long history of deeply rooted traditions, it is also a country that has continually reinvented itself. Ancient India was home to some of the greatest innovations in human history, from the discovery of zero to advancements in medicine, astronomy, and mathematics. These early contributions to science and philosophy laid the foundation for modern knowledge. Even today, India remains at the forefront of technological and scientific advancements. The country's space program is a prime example of how India has seamlessly blended its rich tradition with contemporary technology. With cost-effective missions to Mars and the Moon, India has shown that modernity does not have to come at the expense of its traditions. In fact, it is through embracing both that India is able to craft a future that is distinctly its own.

Another common misconception is that India is defined by poverty and inequality. Global media often highlight the stark contrasts between India's rich and poor, presenting a one-dimensional image of the country as one that is plagued by deep poverty and underdevelopment. While it is undeniable that poverty remains a significant challenge, this oversimplified view fails to acknowledge the complex realities of India. India is home to one of the largest and fastest-growing middle classes in the world. In its urban centers, you'll find thriving industries, world-class infrastructure, and a booming service economy. Cities like Bengaluru, Gurgaon, and Pune are not only global tech hubs but also centers of finance, education, and healthcare. Moreover, the country has made remarkable strides in reducing poverty over the last few decades. According to the World Bank, India lifted over 270 million people out of poverty between 2005 and 2015. The government has implemented various welfare schemes to provide affordable housing, healthcare, and education to millions of people. These initiatives have made a significant impact on the lives of India's poorest citizens, offering them opportunities to escape the cycle of poverty and lead more prosperous lives.

The misconception that India is solely defined by its poverty ignores the thriving economy, rapidly growing sectors, and flourishing middle class that are transforming the country into an economic powerhouse. India's young population is another key factor in its economic growth. With one of the largest and youngest workforces in the world, India is increasingly becoming a global leader in technology and innovation. The global recognition of Indian entrepreneurs, such as Sundar Pichai, Satya Nadella, and Indra Nooyi, further highlights the potential of India's human capital.

India is also often misunderstood as a country with a single, homogenous culture. The country's diversity, in terms of language, religion, and customs, is one of its most defining features, yet it is frequently overlooked. India is a land of over 2,000 languages, hundreds of dialects, and a vast array of cultural practices. Each region in India has its own unique way of life, from the food people eat to the festivals they celebrate. Northern India and southern India, for example, have distinct languages, cuisines, and cultural traditions. The languages spoken in the northeast differ vastly from those in the west or the south. India's religious diversity is equally vast, with followers of Hinduism, Islam, Christianity, Sikhism, Buddhism, and many other religions coexisting peacefully. However, this diversity is often ignored in the global discourse, which tends to present India as a monolithic entity.

Rather than being a source of division, India's diversity is its strength. It is through this diversity that India has fostered an inclusive society where people from various backgrounds can live and thrive together. India's diverse cultural fabric is woven together by a shared sense of belonging, even though the threads themselves may differ significantly. This diversity is reflected in India's festivals, cuisine, music, and even its educational system, which is influenced by multiple cultural traditions. The pluralistic nature of India is not a source of fragmentation but rather a testament to the country's ability to accommodate differences and thrive as a unified whole.

The misconception that India is a country of religious extremism is another deeply entrenched stereotype. While the world has witnessed instances of communal violence in India, such as the Gujarat riots or the conflicts in Kashmir, these events are often blown out of proportion and do not represent the broader social fabric of the country. India is a country that has long been home to people of many faiths, and religious pluralism has been a core principle of Indian society for centuries. The Constitution of India guarantees the freedom of religion and recognizes India as a secular state, ensuring that all religious communities can practice their faith without fear of persecution.

In fact, India's greatest strength lies in its ability to maintain religious harmony despite its diversity. Across the country, you will find examples of religious communities living together peacefully. Hindu temples and Muslim mosques often coexist side by side in the same neighborhoods, and religious festivals from various faiths are celebrated with enthusiasm by people from all communities. India's cultural history is marked by a long tradition of religious tolerance, from the Mughal era's promotion of Hindu-Muslim unity to the peaceful coexistence of Sikhs, Jains, and Buddhists with their Hindu neighbors.

The misconception that India is technologically backward is also a glaring oversight. India is a global leader in technology, especially in the fields of software, information technology, and space exploration. The country has become a hub for IT services, with companies like TCS, Infosys, and Wipro providing services to clients around the world. India's space program is internationally renowned, with successful missions to Mars and the Moon, as well as the launch of numerous satellites for other countries. These achievements are a testament to the fact that India is not only keeping pace with the modern world but also leading the charge in key areas of technological development. India's startups are thriving, and its young entrepreneurs are making their mark on the global stage. The tech industry, coupled with advancements in areas like artificial intelligence, biotechnology, and renewable energy, shows that India is on the cutting edge of modern science and technology.

Lastly, India's population is often portrayed as a burden, with overpopulation seen as a major obstacle to progress. While it is true that India's large population presents challenges, such as overcrowded cities and strained resources, it also presents an opportunity. India has one of the youngest populations in the world, with over 60% of its population under the age of 35. This demographic advantage means that India has a vast and growing workforce that is capable of driving the country's economic development for decades to come.

India's population is also diverse in terms of education, skills, and aspirations. The country boasts some of the best educational institutions in the world, including the Indian Institutes of Technology (IITs) and the Indian Institutes of Management (IIMs), which produce some of the brightest minds globally. India's workforce is highly competitive and increasingly integrated into the global economy, making it a key player in global trade and development. Rather than being a liability, India's population is a major asset, contributing to the country's growth and success.

In conclusion, the global misconceptions about India are deeply rooted in stereotypes and misunderstandings. India is often seen through a narrow lens, one that ignores the country's vast diversity, its achievements in modernity, and its deep cultural heritage. By dispelling these myths, we can foster a deeper understanding of India, a nation that is both ancient and modern, traditional and innovative. India's future lies in its ability to continue embracing its heritage while adapting to the demands of the modern world, and it is through this dynamic synthesis that India will continue to shine on the global stage.

MODERNITY IN CONTEXT OF INDIAN TRADITIONS

Modernity is often seen as a force that changes societies, bringing in new technologies, ideas, and ways of life. However, for India, modernity is not about abandoning the past; it's about finding ways to blend progress with tradition. Understanding modernity in the context of Indian traditions is essential to fully appreciating how India has grown over the years while still remaining deeply rooted in its cultural heritage.

In many parts of the world, modernity is associated with Westernization. People often believe that to be modern, a society must adopt Western values, technologies, and lifestyles. This has led to a perception that modernity in India is about rejecting its age-old customs in favor of something "newer" and "better." However, India has always had its own path to modernity, one that respects and builds upon its traditions.

The Role of Tradition in India's Modern Identity

India's traditions are not mere relics of the past. They form the foundation upon which India's modern identity stands. Traditions like respect for elders, the importance of family and community, and values of non-violence and coexistence shape the way Indians engage with the world, even in a globalized, technologically advanced society.

Take, for example, the Indian family system. The joint family structure, where multiple generations live under one roof, has been an integral part of Indian society for centuries. While it may seem outdated to some, this family model continues to play a significant role in modern India. It is based on the values of mutual care, respect, and shared responsibility. In today's India, even as nuclear families become more common, the value of family still holds great importance. The tradition of looking after the elderly, for example, is still seen as a fundamental duty in Indian society.

This strong sense of family and community can be found in the way modern India approaches challenges. During times of crisis, like the COVID-19 pandemic, many Indians turned to their families for emotional support and assistance. While the world shifted toward digital connections, India's deep-rooted family values helped people feel connected even when physically apart. These values, rooted in tradition, helped people stay grounded and resilient, showing how tradition plays a vital role in modern life.

Modernity as an Evolution of Tradition, Not a Rejection of It

In India, modernization has been a gradual process that involves evolving traditions to meet the demands of the changing world. India's education system, for instance, has undergone massive changes over the years, but it still retains elements of ancient knowledge systems. The Gurukul system of education, which focused on holistic learning, has evolved into today's educational institutions. However, the value of imparting wisdom, teaching respect for knowledge, and fostering personal growth remains the same.

India has also embraced modern technology without letting go of its cultural identity. The country is known for its thriving IT industry, which is one of the largest in the world. Companies like Infosys, TCS, and Wipro have made India a global technology leader. Yet, even in this fast-paced digital world, India's ancient traditions such as yoga, meditation, and Ayurveda are becoming global phenomena. These traditions, grounded in thousands of years of wisdom, have found new relevance in the modern world, especially in areas like health, wellness, and mindfulness.

In a world dominated by consumerism, the idea of simple living and self-contentment—values that have long been a part of Indian philosophy—has found a new audience globally. Modern technology has enabled people around the world to reconnect with these ancient values. India's ability to adapt and reinterpret its traditions to suit modern needs is a significant part of its progress.

How India's Spiritual Traditions Shape Its Modern Approach

India's spiritual traditions are another example of how the country blends the old with the new. For centuries, India has been a spiritual hub, with philosophies like Hinduism, Buddhism, Jainism, and Sikhism offering teachings on peace, non-violence, and self-realization. These traditions are not just about religious practices but also about leading a meaningful and ethical life. In modern times, these values have found applications in various fields such as mental health, stress management, and even business ethics.

One of the most well-known aspects of Indian spirituality is yoga. Although yoga has been practiced in India for thousands of years, it has become a global movement in the past few decades. People from all over the world now practice yoga not just for physical fitness but for mental peace and emotional well-being. This global spread of yoga is a perfect example of how an ancient tradition can evolve and fit into the needs of the modern world. Yoga, like many other aspects of Indian culture, doesn't require a person to abandon modern life; it simply offers tools to live better within it.

India's philosophy of Dharma, or righteous living, is another important tradition that holds great relevance today. Dharma is not limited to religious duties but encompasses ethical conduct, respect for nature, and social responsibility. In modern times, this concept has been adapted to address issues like environmental conservation, corporate responsibility, and social justice. In today's world, where climate change and social inequality are pressing issues, India's traditional values offer important insights on how to live in harmony with nature and society.

Modernity in India's Economic Growth

India's rapid economic growth in recent decades offers another example of how the country's traditions and modernity work together. India's traditional industries, such as textiles, agriculture, and handicrafts, have grown and evolved to meet modern market demands. These sectors, once seen as outdated, are now thriving due to innovations in technology and business practices.

At the same time, India's burgeoning service sector—especially in IT, software, and outsourcing—has made it a global economic player. Yet, the principles that guide India's economic growth are rooted in its traditional values of hard work, entrepreneurship, and resilience. The entrepreneurial spirit, a value that has existed in India for centuries, is seen in the rise of countless startups across the country. Many young entrepreneurs today are using traditional knowledge, resources, and crafts to build innovative businesses. By combining traditional skills with modern technologies, they are creating new avenues of growth.

Moreover, India's agricultural sector, which supports a large portion of the population, has also embraced modern practices without abandoning its cultural traditions. For example, farmers are now using new technology to improve crop yields, while still adhering to sustainable farming methods that have been passed down through generations. This blend of traditional practices with modern innovations has made India's agricultural sector more resilient and self-sustaining.

The Global Impact of India's Tradition-Modernity Balance

India's unique ability to balance tradition with modernity has had a profound impact globally. As the world becomes more interconnected, people from different cultures are increasingly looking to India for guidance on how to navigate the challenges of modern life while staying true to their cultural roots. India's tradition of respect for diversity, non-violence, and coexistence offers valuable lessons for the world, especially in today's divided and fragmented societies.

India's model of progress shows that modernity does not need to erase tradition. Instead, tradition can serve as a solid foundation upon which to build a modern, progressive society. The country's experience teaches us that it is possible to honor the past while embracing the future. In fact, it is the very richness of India's traditions that has allowed it to adapt and thrive in the face of modern challenges.

THE FOUNDATION OF INDIAN TRADITIONS

CHAPTER FOUR

ANCIENT INDIA – A LAND OF WISDOM

India is often called the cradle of civilization, a place where rich and diverse traditions have been passed down through thousands of years. These traditions, deeply rooted in philosophy, art, and culture, form the very backbone of Indian society today. To truly understand the harmonious blend of tradition and modernity that defines India, we must first look back to its ancient history, where the seeds of these enduring values were sown.

The Roots of Indian Traditions

The story of Indian traditions begins in ancient times, with the early civilizations that flourished on the banks of the Indus River. The *Indus Valley Civilization* (around 3300–1300 BCE) is one of the oldest in the world, known for its advanced urban planning, drainage systems, and evidence of trade networks stretching to Mesopotamia.

While much of the language and culture of this civilization remains a mystery, its influence on India's future growth and development cannot be understated.

However, it is with the arrival of the *Vedic period* (around 1500 BCE) that India's spiritual and cultural foundations began to take shape in a way that continues to impact its identity today. The *Vedas*, a collection of ancient hymns, rituals, and philosophical texts, are among the oldest written scriptures in the world. These texts form the core of Hinduism and laid the foundation for many of the values that continue to shape Indian society, such as the concepts of *dharma* (duty), *karma* (action), *moksha* (liberation), and *ahimsa* (non-violence).

Core Indian Values: A Legacy of Wisdom

Indian philosophy, embedded in the teachings of the *Vedas* and *Upanishads*, emphasizes the unity of all life and the importance of ethical conduct. These core values are not mere abstract ideas; they are lived experiences that have guided the actions of individuals and communities for millennia. Let's look at some of the most influential values that have shaped Indian life:

Dharma (Duty): The concept of dharma has its roots in the Vedic texts. It refers to one's ethical duty or moral responsibility in life. Unlike Western ideas of law or morality, dharma is a dynamic, context-based principle, ensuring that an individual's actions are in harmony with the universe. The great epics, the *Mahabharata* and the *Ramayana*, exemplify dharma in action. For instance, the character of Lord Rama in the Ramayana embodies dharma by fulfilling his duties as a son, a husband, and a king, even at great personal cost.

Karma (Action and Consequences): The idea of karma is central to Indian spirituality and practical living. It posits that every action, whether good or bad, creates a chain of consequences. This philosophy encourages personal responsibility and ethical living, as individuals are accountable for their actions. Today, the concept of karma resonates globally, influencing movements related to social justice and ethics.

Ahimsa (Non-Violence): Perhaps one of the most well-known principles from Indian tradition is ahimsa, or non-violence. This concept, preached by great leaders such as Mahatma Gandhi, is a cornerstone of Indian philosophy. Gandhi's use of ahimsa in India's freedom struggle against British rule was not just a political tool but also a powerful, enduring principle that inspires peace movements worldwide.

Seva (Selfless Service): Selfless service, or seva, is another principle rooted in India's traditions. The idea of serving others without expecting anything in return is reflected in the many charitable and social service organizations across India, such as the work done by the Sikh Gurudwaras (places of worship) that serve free meals to anyone who needs them.

These values have been passed down through generations and continue to influence not only Indian society but also the global consciousness, providing answers to some of humanity's most profound questions about duty, morality, and existence.

The Knowledge Systems of Ancient India

Beyond its spiritual and ethical teachings, ancient India was home to some of the world's most remarkable innovations in science, mathematics, and technology. Indian scholars made significant contributions in fields such as astronomy, medicine, and mathematics, laying the groundwork for much of the modern world's scientific achievements.

Mathematics and Astronomy: Ancient Indian mathematicians like Aryabhata and Brahmagupta made groundbreaking discoveries. Aryabhata (476–550 CE) is credited with calculating the value of pi with remarkable precision and proposing that the Earth rotates on its axis. Brahmagupta (598–668 CE) wrote about the concept of zero and negative numbers, which are fundamental to modern mathematics.

Ayurveda and Medicine: Ayurveda, India's ancient system of medicine, is based on the belief that health is a balance between the body, mind, and spirit. This holistic approach has influenced modern alternative medicine and continues to be widely practiced today. Ancient texts like the Charaka Samhita and Sushruta Samhita provide detailed descriptions of surgical procedures, herbal remedies, and medical practices that were far ahead of their time.

Architecture and Engineering: Ancient Indian architecture is renowned for its grandeur and precision. The temples of South India, such as the Brihadeeswarar Temple in Tamil Nadu, are remarkable feats of engineering, built with intricate carvings and remarkable architectural planning. These structures often followed detailed geometric principles that reflect an understanding of math and science that continues to inspire architects today.

The Enduring Influence of Indian Traditions

While ancient India's intellectual contributions are impressive, it is the enduring influence of its cultural and spiritual traditions that continues to guide modern India. The values of dharma, karma, ahimsa, and seva are more than just philosophical ideas—they are practices that shape the way people live, work, and interact with others.

In India today, these values are still evident in daily life. For instance, seva is at the heart of many social service initiatives in the country. The concept of ahimsa continues to shape public discourse on peace, human rights, and environmentalism. And the idea of dharma remains central to the lives of millions, with individuals seeking to align their actions with a sense of moral responsibility, whether in their personal or professional lives.

One of the best examples of this is the concept of "Sustainable Development," which draws heavily on traditional Indian values. Many environmental activists in India draw inspiration from ancient practices of living in harmony with nature, as reflected in texts like the Rigveda, which emphasizes the interconnectedness of all life. India's diverse approach to sustainability—be it in agriculture, architecture, or social practices—is rooted in the ancient belief that humanity must live in balance with the environment.

Personalities Who Embody Ancient Indian Values

Throughout history, several Indian personalities have exemplified the timeless values of ancient India, serving as modern-day ambassadors of tradition:

Mahatma Gandhi: Perhaps the most famous advocate of Indian traditions in the modern world, Gandhi's philosophy of ahimsa and satyagraha (truth-force) was inspired by ancient Indian teachings. His leadership in the Indian independence movement demonstrated how traditional values could be used to bring about significant social and political change.

Dr. B.R. Ambedkar: Ambedkar, the architect of India's Constitution, was deeply influenced by the principles of equality and justice, which have their roots in India's ancient texts. His efforts to uplift the oppressed communities of India were driven by his belief in human dignity, which he saw as central to Indian tradition.

Swami Vivekananda: A key figure in the revival of Hinduism in the late 19th and early 20th centuries, Vivekananda's teachings on spirituality, self-realization, and the unity of all religions echoed the timeless values found in the Vedas and Upanishads. His speech at the 1893 World Parliament of Religions in Chicago highlighted India's deep spiritual tradition while embracing a modern vision of global unity.

CHAPTER FIVE

TRADITIONS AS A GUIDE TO LIFE

India's rich and diverse traditions have long served as a guide to daily living, offering not just cultural identity but also practical wisdom for navigating the complexities of life. At the core of Indian traditions lies the belief that life is a spiritual journey, and it is through the practice of rituals, celebrations, and values that one can find meaning, purpose, and inner peace. Far from being outdated or irrelevant in today's fast-paced world, these traditions offer tools for managing mental health, creating social harmony, and living sustainably. This chapter will explore how traditions—ranging from festivals to daily practices like Ayurveda and yoga—continue to guide and shape Indian society, offering lessons that are more relevant today than ever.

Rituals, Festivals, and Daily Practices: The Meaning Behind the Celebrations

India is a land of festivals—more than 20,000 of them are celebrated annually across the country, reflecting its diversity. Each festival is steeped in centuries-old traditions, often rooted in religious practices, historical events, and seasonal cycles. However, these festivals are not merely about rituals—they serve as an important social and spiritual anchor, fostering community bonding and emotional well-being.

Take, for example, Diwali, the festival of lights. Diwali is celebrated by millions across India and the world, marking the triumph of light over darkness and good over evil. The festival's rituals—lighting oil lamps, bursting fireworks, and cleaning homes—symbolize purification, renewal, and the dispelling of negativity. But beyond the glitter and excitement, Diwali serves as a reminder of the importance of inner light and clarity. For many, it is an opportunity for introspection, forgiveness, and the strengthening of family and community ties.

Similarly, Holi, the festival of colors, is not just about throwing colored powder and celebrating with friends; it is a celebration of unity, inclusiveness, and the joy of life. It encourages people to shed their egos and prejudices, embracing one another without distinction. In a world increasingly divided by social and political lines, festivals like Holi offer a potent reminder of how traditions can help transcend differences and promote social harmony.

Such festivals are not isolated events; they are part of the fabric of daily life in India. People's daily routines are deeply connected to traditions—whether it's the practice of offering prayers in the morning, the importance of family gatherings, or following specific dietary restrictions based on religious teachings. These traditions are not just symbolic; they are guides for maintaining a sense of balance, peace, and well-being in an often chaotic world.

The Wisdom of Ayurveda, Yoga, and Meditation: Ancient Practices for Modern Wellness

At the heart of Indian tradition lies a holistic approach to health and well-being—one that integrates the mind, body, and spirit. Ayurveda, the ancient system of medicine, is one of the oldest forms of healthcare in the world. It teaches that health is not just the absence of disease but a state of balance between the body, mind, and environment. Ayurveda's personalized approach to health emphasizes diet, lifestyle, and natural remedies, offering solutions tailored to an individual's unique constitution.

In recent years, the global popularity of Ayurveda has surged, particularly as people around the world search for alternative, natural remedies to combat stress, anxiety, and chronic illnesses. According to a report by the World Health Organization (WHO), Ayurveda and traditional Indian medicine are gaining recognition globally for their role in holistic wellness. In the United States alone, the market for Ayurvedic products is expected to reach $16 billion by 2026. The integration of Ayurvedic principles with modern medicine in wellness centers across the world highlights the growing appreciation for this ancient tradition.

Similarly, yoga, an integral part of Indian spirituality and health, has become a global phenomenon. From its origins as a spiritual practice in the ancient texts of the Yoga Sutras to its evolution into a physical exercise routine, yoga has transformed into a billion-dollar global industry. The United Nations proclaimed International Yoga Day in 2014, recognizing the physical, mental, and spiritual benefits of yoga. In India, yoga is still practiced by millions every day as a way to maintain health, find inner peace, and deepen one's spiritual connection.

Meditation, too, has found a global audience. With increasing rates of mental health issues such as depression and anxiety, meditation practices like mindfulness and *Vipassana* (originating in India) have become popular tools for reducing stress and improving mental well-being. A 2018 study published in the Journal of Clinical Psychology found that mindfulness meditation can significantly reduce symptoms of anxiety and depression. In India, meditation is still practiced by millions as a way to find clarity and peace amidst the noise of daily life.

Preserving Wisdom for Future Generations: A Timeless Tradition

Indian traditions are not just important in the present—they offer valuable lessons for the future. By passing down wisdom from one generation to the next, these traditions ensure that individuals and communities remain rooted in values that promote well-being, resilience, and social harmony.

The concept of *Guru-Shishya Parampara*, the teacher-student tradition, is a central aspect of India's educational system. In ancient India, knowledge was passed down orally from teacher to student, with a strong emphasis on personal guidance, ethical values, and moral development. Even today, this tradition is present in the way knowledge is shared in family settings and local communities, where elders impart life lessons to younger generations. In today's world, where education is often impersonal and driven by technology, the Guru-Shishya tradition offers a deeply human, value-based approach to learning.

In the same vein, the Indian family system, with its emphasis on respect for elders and intergenerational ties, serves as a model for preserving cultural wisdom. Elders in Indian families often hold the collective memory of the family's traditions, values, and practices, passing them down through stories, teachings, and rituals. These familial bonds serve as emotional and cultural anchors, especially in today's fast-paced, individualistic society.

The Importance of Social Practices: Strengthening Community and Bonding

India's social fabric is intricately woven with traditions that promote unity, collective well-being, and social responsibility. Practices like seva (selfless service), which encourages individuals to work for the benefit of others, have always been deeply embedded in Indian society. The concept of karma, or action, teaches that one's actions, whether big or small, can have a ripple effect on the community and the world.

During the *Kumbh Mela*, the world's largest religious gathering, millions of Hindus gather every year to bathe in the holy rivers of India. Beyond the religious significance, the event is a powerful example of how Indian traditions bring people together in a shared spirit of devotion, unity, and collective action. Volunteers work tirelessly to manage the logistics, provide food and medical assistance, and ensure the safety of the pilgrims. This spirit of service and community is a cornerstone of Indian life and continues to inspire people around the world to work for the greater good.

Volunteerism and community-driven efforts like the *Swachh Bharat Abhiyan* (Clean India Mission), initiated by the Indian government, draw upon the age-old practice of communal responsibility. This modern campaign, which encourages citizens to take pride in maintaining cleanliness in their surroundings, reflects the Indian belief in the importance of self-discipline and collective effort for the greater good.

The traditions of India are not relics of the past but vital, living practices that guide people through the challenges of today's world. From the wisdom of Ayurveda and yoga to the social practices of seva and community service, India's traditions offer practical tools for living a balanced, healthy, and meaningful life. They provide a moral compass and a sense of connection to one's heritage, helping people navigate the complexities of modern existence without losing sight of who they are and where they come from.

In a rapidly changing world, where technology and globalization often lead to a loss of personal connection and spiritual grounding, India's traditions offer much-needed guidance. They remind us of the importance of maintaining harmony within ourselves, with others, and with the environment. As the world faces new challenges—from environmental crises to mental health issues—India's rich cultural heritage offers timeless wisdom that can inspire individuals and societies to move forward while staying rooted in the values that have sustained humanity for millennia.

THE MODERN INDIAN SPIRIT

CHAPTER SIX

REDEFINING MODERNITY – WHAT DOES IT MEAN TO BE MODERN?

Modernity is often defined by the visible markers of technological advancement, urbanization, and economic progress. It's about fast-paced lives, global connectivity, consumerism, and the appearance of being "up-to-date" with the rest of the world. However, this definition, especially in the context of India, falls short of capturing the full essence of what modernity can truly mean. India, with its vast and varied traditions, offers a broader and deeper interpretation of modernity—one that harmonizes the wisdom of the past with the needs and opportunities of the future.

The Need for a New Definition of Modernity

In the globalized world we live in today, modernity is often equated with embracing Western values—consumerism, individualism, and technological supremacy. This version of modernity, which emphasizes material progress, can sometimes seem to clash with India's deep-rooted traditions, which value community, family, spirituality, and sustainable living. But to define modernity through such a narrow lens is to overlook the rich history of Indian innovation and its ongoing potential for social, intellectual, and technological leadership.

Modernity, in the Indian context, is about embracing progress while staying deeply rooted in values that have stood the test of time. It is not just about having the latest technology or following global fashion trends; it is about thinking innovatively, maintaining ethical grounding, and adapting to change without losing the essence of one's cultural identity.

The Old and the New – Finding Common Ground

India has always had a unique approach to integrating the old and the new. Take the example of India's cultural heritage in science and technology. For instance, the concept of zero, an integral part of mathematics today, was first introduced by Indian mathematician Brahmagupta in the 7th century. His groundbreaking work laid the foundation for modern mathematics and computing. Similarly, ancient Indian systems like Ayurveda, which have been practiced for thousands of years, continue to have a profound impact on modern wellness trends globally. Indian culture's inherent flexibility and openness to blending the old with the new has made it possible for the country to remain culturally strong while embracing modernization.

Indian modernity, therefore, is an approach that marries the best of both worlds—the timeless wisdom of tradition and the boundless possibilities of innovation. It is the ability to respect the past while taking steps toward the future, to adapt and evolve, not by abandoning what we were, but by building upon what we have.

Reinterpreting Modernity Through Indian Lenses

The notion of modernity in India isn't just confined to external markers like technological development; it also includes the ability to think critically, embrace diversity, and promote sustainability. Modernity, in an Indian context, often draws from the ancient concept of dharma, which is rooted in the idea of living ethically and in harmony with the universe. This concept influences how we approach the modern challenges of climate change, inequality, and global conflict.

Modernity should not be seen merely as the adoption of external standards but as a self-reflective process of growth that aligns with one's values. As India continues to grow as a global player in the fields of technology, economics, and culture, it is vital that modernity in India also aligns with the principles that make it unique, such as community, collective well-being, and respect for the environment.

Indians Leading the Way in Modernity While Embracing Tradition

Ratan Tata, the former chairman of Tata Group, is an excellent example of how an Indian can be both modern and deeply traditional. Tata is known not just for his successful business ventures, but for the ethical principles that have guided his career. Under his leadership, Tata Group became a global conglomerate, yet Tata has always maintained a focus on values such as integrity, trust, and social responsibility. For instance, Tata Motors' acquisition of Jaguar Land Rover in 2008 was a bold move into the global market, yet Tata ensured that this expansion didn't compromise the company's ethical standards.

Ratan Tata's commitment to ethical business practices and his continued focus on contributing to society shows that one can embrace modern business strategies while staying true to traditional Indian values of service, honesty, and respect for people. In Tata's case, modernity and tradition don't exist in opposition; they complement and strengthen one another.

Sundar Pichai, the CEO of Google, embodies the essence of modernity fused with traditional Indian values. Pichai, who was born and raised in Chennai, India, carries with him the lessons of humility, discipline, and community that are deeply ingrained in Indian culture. As he rose through the ranks at Google, Pichai's approach was always rooted in respect for others and the ability to listen and adapt—qualities that reflect India's traditional values of collaboration and humility.

Despite his global stature, Pichai has often spoken about how his upbringing in India shaped his leadership style. He holds a deep respect for education, which is a key value in

Indian society, and he continues to advocate for accessible education and inclusivity. His success story highlights how modern leadership in the tech world can be inspired by traditional Indian values of community, respect, and hard work.

Indra Nooyi, the former CEO of PepsiCo, offers another remarkable example of an Indian leader who embodies modernity while staying rooted in tradition. Nooyi, born in Chennai, India, grew up with values of discipline, responsibility, and respect for her heritage. As CEO of PepsiCo, she led the company to unprecedented growth, yet she also championed sustainability, community outreach, and health-conscious business practices—values deeply rooted in India's ancient teachings of harmony with nature and well-being.

Nooyi's leadership style blends the best of modern business acumen with a strong belief in traditional Indian family values, the importance of balance in life, and ethical decision-making. Her success in breaking barriers in the corporate world while staying grounded in her heritage speaks to the ability of modern Indians to balance innovation with their cultural roots.

Dr. A.P.J. Abdul Kalam, the former President of India and a renowned aerospace scientist, is one of the most iconic figures who embodies the fusion of modernity with Indian tradition. Known as the "Missile Man of India," Dr. Kalam's contributions to India's space and defense programs were groundbreaking. Yet, his approach to modern science was always rooted in Indian values of spirituality, humility, and service to society.

Throughout his life, Dr. Kalam emphasized the importance of values like integrity and compassion, which he believed were integral to leadership. His vision of India's future, articulated in his book India 2020, combined modern technological growth with a deep reverence for India's cultural traditions and spiritual wisdom. He often referred to ancient Indian texts like the Bhagavad Gita and Upanishads, demonstrating how modern technological advancement and traditional wisdom could coexist to build a strong, forward-looking nation.

His insistence on education, humility, and ethical leadership in the face of modern technological challenges has made him an inspiration to millions of young Indians.

Amitabh Bachchan, one of the most famous actors in the history of Indian cinema, embodies both the modern and traditional aspects of Indian culture. He is considered the "Shahenshah" (Emperor) of Bollywood and is known for his deep voice, commanding presence, and timeless appeal. While Bachchan has redefined the very nature of Indian cinema, he has done so with a strong sense of humility, respect for his roots, and a connection to the broader cultural landscape of India.

In his personal and professional life, Bachchan has always honored traditional Indian values, from his respect for family to his commitment to social causes. Yet, his work in Bollywood also reflects a modern sensibility—embracing change, technological advancement, and new storytelling methods. Whether it is his role in classic films or his presence on the popular TV show Kaun Banega Crorepati (KBC), Bachchan has managed to remain relevant to multiple generations, bridging the gap between old-world charm and modern appeal.

Bachchan's legacy shows that one can embody the values of both tradition and modernity without compromising on authenticity.

Modernity Through Indian Institutions

India has become a hub for startups and social enterprises, many of which combine modern business practices with traditional values. Companies like Amul (a dairy cooperative) and Barefoot College (an NGO that trains women to become solar engineers) show how modern ideas of entrepreneurship can be rooted in traditional community values. These businesses have embraced technology and innovation but are also deeply committed to local empowerment, social responsibility, and sustainability.

Startups in India are increasingly focused on addressing social and environmental issues, aligning with the traditional Indian belief in seva (selfless service). For example, Selco India provides solar energy solutions to rural households, empowering people in underserved areas while ensuring environmental sustainability.

Indian institutions, such as the Indian Institutes of Technology (IITs) and Indian Institutes of Management (IIMs), have contributed significantly to the country's modernization while still emphasizing the importance of ethics and social responsibility. IIT graduates, for instance, are not just skilled in technology but are often taught to think critically, act ethically, and contribute positively to society. The emphasis on holistic education in these institutions reflects the ancient Indian tradition of Vidyā (knowledge) being not just about acquiring facts, but understanding the deeper essence of life.

A Vision for Modern India

Modernity in India should not be seen merely as imitation or adoption of external ideals, but as the evolution of a culture that has thrived for thousands of years. To be truly modern is to integrate innovation with tradition, technology with sustainability, and individual success with collective well-being. India's path to modernity can serve as a model for other nations, demonstrating that growth and development are not just about technological advancements, but also about staying true to the values that guide us as individuals and as a society.

As India moves forward on its development journey, it must continue to honor its heritage while embracing modernity in a way that respects the environment, promotes social harmony, and enables personal growth. In this ever-changing world, the Indian way of blending tradition with progress offers a vision of modernity that is inclusive, sustainable, and ethical.

CHAPTER SEVEN

MODERN INNOVATION INSPIRED BY TRADITION

In today's fast-paced world, the idea of tradition often seems at odds with progress and innovation. Yet, India's unique ability to blend the two is a testimony to its capacity for transformation while staying true to its roots. While the world often sees India as a land steeped in ancient customs and rituals, it is also a vibrant hub of modern innovation, technology, and entrepreneurship. Interestingly, much of this modern success is built on the foundation of India's rich traditions, which continue to inspire the country's technological, scientific, and cultural advancements.

Traditional Knowledge as the Foundation of Modern Innovation

One of the most fascinating aspects of India's growth story is how its traditional knowledge has fueled some of its most significant innovations. This is particularly true in the fields of agriculture, medicine, and engineering, where ancient practices have laid the groundwork for modern solutions. Let's explore how India's traditional wisdom has become a key driver of innovation.

Sustainable Agriculture: Ancient Practices in Modern Times

Agriculture has always been at the heart of India's economy, and its traditional farming techniques have been remarkably sustainable. For centuries, Indian farmers have used natural methods to cultivate crops in harmony with the environment. Practices like crop rotation, organic composting, and rainwater harvesting have been part of the Indian agricultural landscape for thousands of years.

Take, for example, the Zero Budget Natural Farming (ZBNF) method pioneered by Subhash Palekar. ZBNF is a farming practice that draws heavily on ancient Indian methods of organic farming, which do not rely on costly chemical fertilizers or pesticides. This system emphasizes the use of local resources and biodiversity, focusing on soil health and natural growth processes.

Palekar's work has gained widespread attention and has been implemented in various states across India, providing a model for sustainable farming. In fact, the government of India has even recognized ZBNF as a potential solution to the growing concerns about soil degradation and chemical overuse in agriculture.

In addition, traditional techniques such as rainwater harvesting, practiced in Rajasthan's Johad system, have been modernized to address the challenges of water scarcity. The Johad system, which involves building small ponds to capture rainwater, has been revived in several parts of India and is contributing significantly to groundwater replenishment.

India's use of traditional farming techniques combined with modern agricultural innovations has created a model for sustainable farming, which is now being studied and adopted in other parts of the world.

Ayurveda and Modern Medicine: A Timeless Connection

India's medical traditions, particularly Ayurveda, have always been ahead of their time in terms of holistic care. Ayurveda, which dates back over 5,000 years, is a system of medicine that focuses on maintaining the balance between the body, mind, and spirit. The ancient texts of Ayurveda contain knowledge about herbal medicines, detoxification processes, and preventive healthcare.

While modern science and medicine have evolved in parallel, Ayurveda continues to influence contemporary healthcare practices. In fact, the integration of Ayurvedic principles into modern medicine is gaining significant attention. Many modern wellness and healthcare companies are now blending Ayurvedic wisdom with Western medicine, focusing on holistic treatments and preventive care.

One of the most well-known examples of Ayurveda's influence on modern innovation is the rise of Ayurvedic products in the global wellness market. Companies like Patanjali, Dabur, and Himalaya have built successful empires by combining Ayurvedic knowledge with modern production techniques. These brands are now household names not only in India but across the world, with products ranging from skincare and haircare to digestive aids and supplements.

Moreover, Ayurvedic medicines are being integrated into the global pharmaceutical industry. The World Health Organization (WHO) has acknowledged the importance of traditional medicine, including Ayurveda, in its global strategy for traditional medicine 2014-2023. The increasing demand for natural, plant-based remedies is prompting pharmaceutical companies worldwide to explore Ayurvedic formulations for conditions like stress, anxiety, and digestive issues.

Creativity in Art, Culture, and Entrepreneurship

India's arts and cultural traditions are another significant source of modern innovation. From classical dance and music to literature and film, Indian culture continues to inspire creative minds around the world. Today, many artists and entrepreneurs are breathing new life into these traditions, finding ways to modernize and globalize them while preserving their essence.

Modern Artists and Cultural Revival

Take the world of Indian classical dance as an example. Classical dance forms like Bharatanatyam, Kathak, Odissi, and Kathakali have been practiced in India for centuries. These art forms are rooted in religious and cultural rituals and have been passed down through generations. Yet, contemporary artists are redefining these traditional performances by blending them with modern storytelling, multimedia elements, and even western dance forms.

One such artist is Shobana, a renowned Bharatanatyam dancer who has been instrumental in popularizing the art form globally. She has combined Bharatanatyam with Western ballet, creating unique performances that resonate with international audiences. Shobana's work shows how tradition and modernity can come together to create something new and exciting, without losing the cultural significance of the art.

Similarly, in the world of Indian cinema, Bollywood has taken its traditional storytelling methods and combined them with the latest technological advancements in filmmaking. Filmmakers are now using cutting-edge technology like CGI and 3D animation alongside traditional Indian motifs and themes. The success of films like Baahubali and RRR is evidence of how Indian cinema is embracing modern technology while staying true to its cultural roots. These films have not only broken box office records in India but have gained international recognition, showing the world that India's traditional storytelling methods can compete on the global stage.

Indian Entrepreneurship and Innovation

Entrepreneurship in India is another area where tradition meets modernity. Many modern Indian entrepreneurs have drawn inspiration from the values and philosophies embedded in India's traditional culture. For instance, the concept of seva (selfless service) has influenced the way many businesses are run today. Rather than focusing solely on profits, several successful Indian entrepreneurs are now building companies with a strong emphasis on social impact.

Ratan Tata, the former chairman of Tata Group, is a prime example of a business leader who integrates traditional values with modern business practices. Under his leadership, Tata Group became one of India's most respected companies, known not only for its business acumen but also for its commitment to social causes. Tata's approach to business is rooted in the Indian tradition of dharma (duty), where doing good for society is seen as an integral part of a business's success.

Furthermore, India's start-up ecosystem is booming, with young entrepreneurs using technology to solve problems rooted in India's traditional ways of life. Byju Raveendran, the founder of Byju's, has taken traditional methods of learning and combined them with modern technology, creating a global edtech giant that is revolutionizing how students learn across the world. Byju's success story is a perfect example of how modern innovation can be built on the foundation of traditional educational values, such as discipline, hard work, and knowledge.

Global Impact: India as a Leader in Tradition-Driven Innovation

India's global influence continues to grow, not only in terms of its economy and technology but also in cultural and societal contributions. The world is increasingly recognizing India's ability to blend tradition with modernity, leading to a greater appreciation for its cultural and intellectual contributions.

For example, Yoga and Meditation—two practices deeply rooted in Indian tradition—have become a global phenomenon. Celebrities, athletes, and everyday people around the world are turning to these practices for physical and mental well-being. India's ancient teachings on mindfulness and balance are being embraced in schools, workplaces, and health clubs across the globe. The International Day of Yoga, recognized by the United Nations since 2015, is a testament to the global impact of India's spiritual heritage.

Additionally, India's commitment to sustainability and green technology is increasingly drawing from traditional values. The country's focus on renewable energy, sustainable farming, and eco-friendly practices is deeply influenced by its cultural respect for nature and the environment. Traditional concepts like ahimsa (non-violence) and prithvi (earth) are being used to promote more sustainable and harmonious living in the modern world.

India's unique ability to blend tradition with modernity has created a powerful foundation for its growth. From sustainable agriculture and holistic healthcare to modern entrepreneurship and global cultural influence, India's traditional knowledge continues to inspire innovation. It proves that progress doesn't have to mean abandoning the past—it can mean reinterpreting the past in a way that propels us forward.

In the years to come, India's example will likely inspire other countries to look inward, to their own cultural and traditional wisdom, and to see it not as a limitation, but as the key to boundless growth and progress.

CHAPTER EIGHT

INDIANS ON THE GLOBAL STAGE

India's global influence has grown substantially over the past few decades, and much of this success lies in the country's ability to blend its rich traditions with modern innovations. Indians, both in India and across the world, have found unique ways to bring their cultural heritage into the global stage while embracing contemporary ideas. This chapter explores how India's global influence is driven by its deep connection to tradition, as well as its innovative spirit.

The Indian Diaspora's Role

One of the most significant contributors to India's global presence is its diaspora. Today, there are approximately 18 million people of Indian origin living outside India, making it one of the largest and most influential global communities. The Indian diaspora, spread across countries like the United States, the United Kingdom, Canada, the Middle East, and Southeast Asia, plays a vital role in shaping the global perception of India.

Indians Abroad: Representing Tradition and Modernity

For the Indian diaspora, the challenge has often been about finding a balance between retaining their cultural roots and integrating into the societies they live in. In doing so, they have showcased India's dual identity: deeply traditional yet incredibly modern. This fusion of old and new can be seen in multiple aspects of life, from work and business to cultural expressions like music, food, and festivals.

For instance, Dr. Venkatraman Ramakrishnan, an Indian-American biochemist, won the Nobel Prize in Chemistry in 2009 for his work on the structure and function of ribosomes. Despite having achieved such recognition on the global stage, Ramakrishnan is rooted in his Indian upbringing. He grew up in India with a deep appreciation for education and science, values that have shaped his successful career. His recognition on the global stage is a testament to how traditional values like respect for education and hard work can seamlessly align with modern achievements.

Another prominent figure is Nina Davuluri, who made history in 2014 by becoming the first Miss America of Indian descent. Growing up in a family that emphasized the importance of cultural heritage, Nina proudly represented her Indian roots while embracing the values of self-expression and empowerment in the United States. Her achievement is symbolic of how Indian traditions and modern global opportunities can merge to create something new.

Another example is Mindy Kaling, an actress, comedian, and writer of Indian descent. Kaling's success in Hollywood as an actress and creator of popular shows like The Mindy Project reflects the intersection of traditional Indian values and contemporary American culture. While her career embodies modernity, Kaling frequently embraces her cultural background in her work, from referencing her Indian heritage to celebrating festivals like Diwali.

This blend of tradition and modernity is not limited to professional lives; it is also reflected in cultural and social expressions. In cities like New York, London, and Toronto, vibrant Indian communities celebrate Diwali, Holi, and other traditional festivals with a modern twist, often blending them with Western elements like music, food, and fashion. Through these celebrations, the diaspora reinforces the idea that modernity does not mean giving up one's cultural heritage—it's about adapting and celebrating both.

Indians Making an Impact Globally

Beyond the realm of business and entertainment, Indians have made significant strides in various sectors around the world, bringing their cultural heritage to the forefront of innovation and progress. Their success stories are a powerful example of how India's traditions have helped shape modern leaders and change-makers.

Sundar Pichai, the CEO of Google, is one such leader who embodies the blend of tradition and modernity. Born and raised in Madurai, India, Pichai's upbringing was steeped in traditional Indian values such as education, discipline, and humility. These values were crucial as he navigated his rise to the top of one of the world's most influential tech companies. Pichai has often spoken about how his Indian upbringing and education shaped his worldview and approach to leadership.

Another prominent example is Satya Nadella, the CEO of Microsoft. Nadella, born in Hyderabad, India, has spoken extensively about how his Indian heritage—especially the values of empathy, learning, and service—shaped his leadership style. Under his leadership, Microsoft has seen significant innovation and transformation, proving that being rooted in tradition and culture does not limit global impact. Nadella's leadership is grounded in the belief that technology should empower people, a philosophy that resonates deeply with the Indian tradition of seva (selfless service).

India's Cultural Influence on the Global Stage

Indian culture has become a significant force globally, particularly in areas like arts, film, and cuisine. Indian cinema, especially Bollywood, has gained immense popularity worldwide. Films like Lagaan (2001) and Dangal (2016) not only showcase Indian culture but also highlight universal themes such as resilience, teamwork, and overcoming adversity—values rooted deeply in Indian traditions.

Bollywood actors such as Priyanka Chopra and Deepika Padukone have achieved global fame, and their work has helped bridge the gap between Indian culture and global entertainment. Priyanka Chopra, in particular, is an excellent example of an Indian artist who has successfully navigated both Bollywood and Hollywood, representing the blend of Indian tradition with Western modernity. Chopra's participation in global events, her success in international TV shows like Quantico, and her advocacy for social causes demonstrate how she integrates her Indian heritage with a globalized lifestyle.

Indian cuisine has also made its mark internationally. Dishes like biryani, samosas, and butter chicken are beloved across the world, but they also represent the intricate, centuries-old culinary traditions of India. Indian chefs and restaurateurs, such as Vikas Khanna and Madhur Jaffrey, have brought traditional Indian cooking to a global audience, infusing modern techniques and ingredients into classic dishes. This fusion has helped Indian food become a staple in many countries, while preserving its authentic flavors and traditions.

Indian classical music and dance forms like Bharatanatyam, Kathak, and Hindustani classical music have found global recognition through performances by artists like Anoushka Shankar (sitar player) and Pandit Ravi Shankar (sitar maestro). These art forms, deeply tied to Indian spirituality and philosophy, are increasingly respected worldwide for their complexity and emotional depth.

India as a Global Leader of Change

As India's economic and political power grows, its role on the global stage continues to expand. India is now one of the world's largest economies, and its influence in global organizations like the United Nations, the World Trade Organization, and BRICS (Brazil, Russia, India, China, South Africa) has grown significantly. India's foreign policy often reflects a deep commitment to peace, stability, and development—values that are at the core of its traditional teachings.

India's leadership in the field of sustainability and environmentalism is a case in point. The traditional Indian philosophy of living in harmony with nature—Vasudhaiva Kutumbakam (the world is one family)—has inspired India's approach to environmental policies. India has been a strong advocate for global climate action, calling for more significant contributions from developed countries to address climate change.

India's growing leadership in renewable energy is another example of the fusion of tradition and modernity. The country has set ambitious targets for solar energy and wind power and is home to the world's largest solar park, in Pavagada, Karnataka. This commitment to renewable energy draws on traditional Indian values of sustainability, while using modern technologies to address the challenges of the 21st century.

India's role as a peacekeeper and advocate for global cooperation has also been shaped by its deep-rooted values of non-violence and diplomacy, inspired by the teachings of figures like Mahatma Gandhi. India's voice on issues such as conflict resolution, global trade, and climate change has grown stronger as the nation balances its cultural heritage with a modern global outlook.

The Role of Indian Culture in Shaping a Modern Future

The global impact of India's diaspora, its leaders, and its cultural exports shows that the ability to blend tradition with modernity is not only possible but essential in today's interconnected world. India's unique approach to modernity—one that does not reject tradition but builds upon it—has become a model for the rest of the world.

As the Indian diaspora continues to grow and prosper, its members are proving that it is possible to be deeply rooted in one's heritage while also engaging with the world in meaningful ways. The success of Indian leaders like Sundar Pichai, Satya Nadella, and Indra Nooyi, as well as the global influence of Indian culture through film, cuisine, and the arts, shows that tradition and modernity can coexist harmoniously.

In the coming years, India's global role will only continue to grow, guided by its deep respect for tradition and its commitment to innovation. The country's ability to stay grounded in its cultural values while embracing the opportunities of a rapidly changing world will be a powerful example for other nations.

TIMELESS TRADITIONS, INFINITE POSSIBILITIES

CHAPTER NINE

EXPANDING HORIZONS

Traditions often seem like a tether to the past, a reminder of old ways and customs. However, for many Indians, traditions are not about staying bound—they are a foundation that provides stability, purpose, and perspective. They help individuals and communities make sense of their place in the world, offering a sense of belonging while broadening their horizons for growth and progress. This dual role of tradition as a stabilizing force and an enabler of innovation is what makes India's cultural fabric so unique.

Traditions as Tools for Personal Growth

India's traditions are built on values that teach personal discipline, resilience, and empathy, forming the heart of its culture. These values are passed down through generations and are a part of everyday life, shaping how people live and interact. They are taught in families, where respect for elders and staying united are important, and in communities, where helping each other is often put before personal needs. Stories from ancient epics, folk tales, and sayings offer lessons on how to live a good and honest life. Festivals and rituals are not just about celebration but also about learning patience, self-control, and care for others. Practices like yoga and meditation help people stay strong and calm while understanding and caring for those around them. Even as the world changes, these values remain strong, finding new ways to fit into modern life. They keep India's rich culture alive and inspire others by showing how tradition can guide a peaceful and balanced life.

The Discipline of Rituals

In Indian households, daily rituals form the foundation of discipline. Many families begin their day with prayers, lighting a lamp, or performing simple offerings to deities. These morning rituals encourage individuals to wake up early, start the day with focus, and express gratitude for life. Such practices create a sense of routine and mindfulness, helping people feel grounded and purposeful.

For instance, the practice of sandhyavandanam, a prayer offered at sunrise and sunset, is rooted in ancient traditions. It reminds individuals to stay in tune with nature's rhythms and take a moment to reflect on their actions. Similarly, rituals like maintaining a clean space for worship encourage tidiness and respect for one's surroundings.

These daily rituals are often small but impactful, teaching the importance of consistency and dedication. Even children who participate in these practices learn the value of routine and responsibility from a young age.

Rituals in Indian traditions also mark significant life events, such as births, marriages, and deaths. These ceremonies are deeply symbolic and often involve intricate steps that must be followed precisely. The discipline required for these rituals reflects their importance and ensures that they are performed with sincerity and respect.

For instance, a wedding ceremony in India involves numerous rituals, each with its own meaning. From the mehendi and haldi ceremonies to the actual wedding rituals like saptapadi (taking seven steps together), every step requires preparation and coordination. These rituals emphasize the importance of family, commitment, and the sanctity of marriage. They also teach patience and the ability to work together during important milestones.

Similarly, rituals performed after the birth of a child, such as namkaran (naming ceremony), bring families together and help them welcome the new member into their cultural and spiritual fold. These rituals, while joyful, also require attention to detail and adherence to traditional practices, instilling discipline in those involved.

Indian rituals are not just personal practices; they often involve entire communities, fostering social discipline and harmony. Festivals like Ganesh Chaturthi or Durga Puja bring neighborhoods together as people collaborate to organize grand celebrations. From setting up pandals (temporary structures) to arranging food and music, every task requires cooperation and coordination.

Such rituals teach individuals to work as a team, respect others' contributions, and follow collective decisions. They also create a sense of accountability, as everyone plays a role in ensuring the success of the event. These community-based rituals strengthen bonds and remind people of the importance of unity and shared responsibilities.

While traditional rituals remain significant, they have also evolved to fit modern lifestyles. Urban families may adapt rituals to suit their schedules, while others use technology to stay connected to their cultural practices. For example, online pujas and virtual celebrations have become popular, allowing people to participate in rituals even when they are far from home.

This adaptability ensures that the discipline of rituals continues to thrive, even as society changes. It also highlights the flexibility of Indian traditions, which evolve without losing their core values.

The Strength of Community Bonds

The strength of community bonds is one of the most defining aspects of Indian society. For centuries, these bonds have been the foundation of India's social structure, providing a sense of belonging, support, and purpose to individuals. Communities in India are not just groups of people living together; they are deeply connected networks that share traditions, values, and responsibilities. These connections create a unique sense of unity and cooperation, allowing people to face life's challenges and celebrate its joys together.

In Indian villages, communities function as extended families. People know each other closely, share resources, and often come together to solve problems or celebrate important occasions. For instance, during weddings, births, or festivals, it is common for the entire village to contribute their time, effort, or resources. This shared responsibility creates a sense of mutual care and strengthens relationships. Everyone plays a role, and no one feels alone, even in times of difficulty. These bonds are not just about helping one another; they also build trust and loyalty, which are essential for the smooth functioning of any society.

Even in cities, where life is faster and more individualistic, community bonds remain strong. Housing societies, apartment complexes, and neighborhood groups often function as smaller communities within urban settings. People gather for festivals, organize social events, and come together to address common concerns, such as cleanliness or safety. This sense of togetherness helps bridge the gap between people who may otherwise live isolated lives in a busy urban environment. In times of need, these communities step forward to provide support, whether it is during a medical emergency or a natural disaster.

Festivals are one of the strongest ways communities bond in India. Celebrations like Diwali, Holi, Eid, Christmas, and Pongal are not just personal events but communal activities. Streets and neighborhoods come alive with decorations, music, and food, as people gather to celebrate together. The preparations and festivities are often collaborative, with everyone pitching in to make the event a success. This shared joy brings people closer and strengthens their connection to one another. Even people from different religions and cultures often join in, reflecting the inclusive nature of Indian communities.

Religious gatherings are another powerful example of strong community bonds in India. Pilgrimages to places like Varanasi, Amritsar, Ajmer, and Sabarimala are not just individual spiritual journeys but collective experiences. People travel together, share meals, and support one another throughout the journey. The sense of belonging and shared faith that these experiences create is unparalleled. It is not uncommon for strangers to form lifelong friendships during such events, bound by the common purpose of faith and devotion.

The tradition of selfless service, or seva, is deeply ingrained in Indian communities and strengthens their bonds further. In many religious and social settings, people come together to help others without expecting anything in return. For example, the concept of langar in Sikhism, where free meals are served to everyone, is a powerful expression of community strength. Volunteers from all walks of life contribute their time and effort to cook and serve food, ensuring no one goes hungry. This act of collective kindness fosters a sense of equality and reinforces the idea that everyone is part of a larger, supportive community.

During times of crisis, the strength of community bonds becomes even more evident. Whether it is a natural disaster like floods or earthquakes or a personal tragedy like a death in the family, communities in India rally together to provide support. Neighbors and friends offer emotional comfort, financial assistance, or practical help, such as preparing meals or arranging logistics. This unwavering support ensures that no one faces hardships alone, creating a safety net that strengthens social resilience.

Indian communities are also instrumental in preserving and passing down traditions, culture, and knowledge. Elders in the community often play a significant role in teaching younger generations about their heritage, values, and customs. Through stories, songs, and rituals, they ensure that the wisdom of the past is not lost. Community celebrations and gatherings act as platforms for this exchange of knowledge, keeping cultural practices alive and relevant. This shared cultural identity helps bind people together, giving them a sense of pride and continuity.

Economic interdependence is another aspect of strong community bonds in India. In rural areas, cooperative farming practices, shared water resources, and collective markets are examples of how communities work together for mutual benefit. Small businesses in towns and cities often rely on community support to thrive, with people preferring to buy from local vendors or craftsmen they know. This economic collaboration not only strengthens community ties but also promotes a sense of shared prosperity.

Modern technology has also played a role in maintaining and enhancing community bonds. Social media platforms, messaging apps, and online forums allow people to stay connected with their communities, even if they are physically distant. Virtual gatherings, online celebrations, and group discussions have become common, especially during times like the COVID-19 pandemic. These digital interactions have shown that the essence of community bonds transcends physical boundaries and can adapt to changing times.

Despite the strength of these bonds, Indian communities are not without challenges. Urbanization, globalization, and individualism have sometimes weakened traditional community structures, leading to a sense of isolation for some individuals. However, the resilience of Indian communities is evident in their ability to adapt and reinvent themselves. New forms of community are emerging, such as professional networks, hobby groups, and social organizations, which continue to provide support and foster connections.

In essence, the strength of community bonds in India lies in their ability to bring people together, offering a sense of belonging and shared purpose. Whether it is through shared celebrations, collective efforts, or mutual support during tough times, these bonds create a strong social fabric that unites individuals across differences. They remind people that they are part of something bigger than themselves, providing strength, comfort, and joy. In a world that is often fast-paced and fragmented, the enduring strength of Indian community bonds stands as a testament to the power of togetherness and cooperation.

Grounding Through Spirituality

Grounding oneself through the diverse philosophies of ancient India reveals a profound understanding of life, reality, and human purpose. These philosophies, encompassing Jainism, Buddhism, Vedanta, Nyaya-Vaisheshika, and other schools of thought, offer unique perspectives on how individuals can connect deeply with themselves and the world around them. Unlike approaches centered on physical or meditative practices, these systems of thought emphasize principles and frameworks that shape the very fabric of one's existence, relying on ancient Sanskrit ideas to guide human conduct and understanding.

Jainism introduces the concept of ahimsa, or non-violence, as a foundation for living a grounded life. This principle extends beyond physical actions to include thoughts and words, emphasizing complete mindfulness in every interaction. Alongside ahimsa, aparigraha, or non-possessiveness, highlights the importance of detachment from material desires. By embracing these values, individuals learn to live with minimal desires and focus on inner wealth rather than external possessions. Jainism's grounding lies in the cultivation of samyama, self-restraint, which fosters harmony and balance within and helps maintain a connection with the broader web of life.

Buddhism, with its concept of pratityasamutpada, or dependent origination, delves into the interconnected nature of existence. It teaches that nothing exists in isolation; every phenomenon arises due to a network of causes and conditions. This realization offers a sense of grounding by reducing attachment and helping individuals accept the impermanence (anitya) of all things. Buddhism further explores the idea of shunyata, or emptiness, which is not a void but the understanding that all things lack inherent existence. Recognizing this emptiness helps individuals transcend illusions (maya) and embrace a reality that is fluid and ever-changing. These teachings inspire a grounded approach to life, where one is not swayed by transient highs and lows but remains centered in an awareness of the present moment.

The Vedantic tradition contributes to this dialogue with its exploration of Brahman, the ultimate reality, and Atman, the inner self. Grounding, according to Vedanta, comes from understanding the unity between the self and the cosmos, as captured in the phrase Tat Tvam Asi (That Thou Art). This realization dissolves the sense of separateness and anchors the individual in a universal consciousness. Vedanta also speaks of viveka (discernment) and vairagya (detachment) as essential tools for achieving this grounded state. Through viveka, one learns to distinguish between the transient and the eternal, while vairagya encourages letting go of fleeting desires and attachments. This path leads to moksha, or liberation, which is not an escape from life but a deep immersion into its most profound truths.

Nyaya and Vaisheshika, ancient schools of logic and metaphysics, provide a unique lens for grounding through knowledge (jnana) and reason (tarka). Nyaya emphasizes the pursuit of valid knowledge (pramana) through observation, inference, and testimony, fostering a grounded understanding of reality. It teaches that clarity of thought and precise reasoning are essential for navigating the complexities of life. Vaisheshika complements this with its focus on categorizing the fundamental elements of existence, such as dravya (substance), guna (qualities), and karma (motion). By understanding these categories and their interactions, individuals gain insight into the structure of the universe and their place within it. This intellectual grounding helps one remain steady and composed, even in the face of uncertainty.

Sankhya philosophy adds to this rich discourse by outlining the interplay between Purusha (consciousness) and Prakriti (matter). It describes a dualistic reality where the grounding of the self arises from recognizing the distinction between these two forces. While Prakriti encompasses the material and ever-changing world, Purusha represents the unchanging, eternal observer. Sankhya teaches that grounding occurs when one aligns with Purusha, transcending the distractions of the material world and realizing the stillness within. This understanding fosters a sense of detachment without disengagement, enabling individuals to navigate life's experiences with clarity and balance.

Ancient Indian philosophies also explore the idea of dharma, a central concept that permeates almost all schools of thought. Dharma represents the moral and ethical duties that sustain harmony in the universe. Living in accordance with one's dharma is seen as a way of staying grounded, as it aligns personal actions with the greater cosmic order. By adhering to dharma, individuals contribute to the well-being of their communities and the world, creating a sense of purpose and connection that anchors them amidst life's uncertainties.

Underlying these philosophies is a shared recognition of the impermanence and interconnectedness of existence. Whether it is through the Jain emphasis on the sanctity of all life, the Buddhist acceptance of life's transient nature, the Vedantic pursuit of universal unity, or the logical inquiry of Nyaya, these ancient systems offer profound insights into what it means to live a grounded life. They remind us that grounding is not about escaping the world but engaging with it fully, guided by principles of wisdom, compassion, and awareness.

Grounding through these philosophies involves a holistic understanding of oneself, others, and the universe. It encourages a life of balance, where actions are guided by ethical principles, and knowledge is sought not for power but for clarity and growth. These teachings, steeped in centuries of wisdom, continue to resonate today, offering timeless guidance for those seeking stability, purpose, and harmony in an ever-changing world.

Wisdom in Indigenous Practices

The revival of traditional practices in modern India has shown how age-old wisdom can address today's pressing issues in practical and sustainable ways. These practices, rooted in the collective knowledge of generations, are finding relevance in areas such as agriculture, water management, architecture, and healthcare. As India faces challenges like climate change, resource scarcity, and environmental degradation, these traditions are being revisited not just for their cultural value but also for the solutions they offer in a rapidly changing world.

One of the most prominent examples of this revival is seen in water conservation. In many parts of ancient India, water was considered sacred, and elaborate systems were created to manage this precious resource sustainably. These systems included stepwells, tanks, and canals designed to harvest rainwater and distribute it efficiently. Inspired by this legacy, modern initiatives like pani panchayats (village water councils) have emerged in states like Maharashtra. These councils encourage communities to manage water collectively, ensuring fair distribution and preventing overuse. By involving local people in decision-making and using traditional water management techniques, villages have been able to combat water scarcity and drought effectively. This approach not only conserves water but also fosters a sense of responsibility and community spirit.

Similarly, traditional farming practices are being embraced as sustainable alternatives to chemical-intensive agriculture. Ancient Indian farmers relied on organic methods, crop rotation, and mixed cropping to maintain soil fertility and ensure food security. These techniques, which avoided synthetic pesticides and fertilizers, are now being reintroduced to counter the harmful effects of modern agricultural practices. States like Sikkim have taken significant steps in this direction, becoming entirely organic by reviving traditional farming methods. This shift not only protects the soil and environment but also provides healthier food for consumers and ensures long-term agricultural sustainability. Across India, more farmers are turning to these methods, inspired by the success of states like Sikkim and the growing awareness of organic produce's benefits.

Traditional architecture has also seen a revival due to its sustainability and energy efficiency. Ancient Indian buildings were designed to adapt to the local climate, using materials like mud, stone, and bamboo. Techniques such as jaalis (perforated screens) for ventilation, courtyards for natural light, and sloping roofs to manage monsoon rains made these structures both comfortable and environmentally friendly. Today, architects are drawing inspiration from these methods to create modern spaces that reduce energy consumption and integrate harmoniously with nature. In urban areas, green building practices, inspired by traditional architecture, are gaining popularity as a response to the environmental impact of concrete-dominated construction.

Healthcare is another area where traditional practices are being revived. Ayurveda, India's ancient system of medicine, has gained global recognition for its holistic approach to health. Ayurveda emphasizes prevention and balance, using natural remedies, diet, and lifestyle changes to treat ailments. In modern India, there has been a resurgence in Ayurvedic treatments and products, with many people turning to these age-old methods for wellness and immunity. The government has also supported this revival by promoting Ayurveda alongside modern medicine, recognizing its potential to complement contemporary healthcare systems.

The revival of traditional textile and craft practices has also contributed to sustainability while preserving India's cultural heritage. Techniques like handloom weaving, natural dyeing, and block printing are being reintroduced to create eco-friendly fashion. These practices, which use minimal energy and resources, are an antidote to the fast fashion industry's environmental damage. Designers and consumers alike are embracing these traditional crafts for their aesthetic value and sustainable impact, providing livelihoods to artisans while reducing the carbon footprint of the textile industry.

In urban areas, traditional food practices are also making a comeback as people recognize their nutritional and environmental benefits. Ancient Indian diets emphasized locally grown, seasonal ingredients and simple cooking methods. This approach minimized waste and ensured that meals were both healthy and sustainable. In recent years, there has been a renewed interest in millets, an ancient grain that is drought-resistant and highly nutritious. States like Karnataka have actively promoted millets, reintroducing them into diets as a solution to both malnutrition and water-intensive crops like rice and wheat.

The revival of traditional practices has also extended to forest and wildlife conservation. Indigenous communities in India have long lived in harmony with nature, following practices that protect biodiversity while meeting their needs. These communities have used methods such as controlled burning to maintain forests, rotational grazing to prevent overuse of pastures, and sacred groves to preserve certain areas of wilderness. Modern conservationists are now collaborating with these communities, recognizing the value of their knowledge in protecting ecosystems and combating climate change.

Education systems are also beginning to integrate traditional knowledge, helping younger generations understand the importance of sustainability and cultural heritage. Schools and colleges in India are introducing courses on organic farming, rainwater harvesting, and renewable energy, often inspired by traditional methods. By combining modern science with ancient wisdom, these programs aim to create a more informed and responsible generation.

This revival is not without challenges. Modern systems and lifestyles often prioritize convenience and speed, which can sometimes clash with the slower, more deliberate nature of traditional practices. Additionally, the knowledge of these practices is often fragmented, as modernization has led to the loss of many traditional skills and techniques. However, efforts are being made to document and revive this knowledge through community projects, government initiatives, and academic research.

The revival of traditional practices in India is more than just a return to the past; it is a way of adapting ancient wisdom to meet modern needs. These practices remind us of the importance of living in harmony with nature and valuing community involvement and long-term thinking. Whether through sustainable farming, water conservation, eco-friendly construction, or holistic healthcare, these traditions offer practical solutions to some of the most pressing problems of our time. By embracing them, India is not only preserving its cultural heritage but also building a more sustainable future.

The Tradition of Seva (Service)

The Indian concept of seva, or selfless service, has been an important part of the country's culture for a long time. It is based on the idea that helping others is a way of finding personal fulfillment and improving society. Seva is not just about giving to those in need; it also focuses on empowering people to become self-sufficient, promoting equality, and helping everyone lead a better life.

One inspiring example of seva in action is the Barefoot College in Rajasthan, which was founded by Bunker Roy. The college follows the Gandhian idea of Gram Swaraj (village self-reliance) and focuses on teaching rural women important skills. At the Barefoot College, women are trained in solar engineering, giving them the ability to provide renewable energy solutions in their own villages. This helps solve two major issues: providing energy to places that lack electricity and promoting gender equality by empowering women with new skills. The program has helped many women become self-sufficient, and the college's work has been recognized worldwide.

The blending of traditional values with modern education is not unique to the Barefoot College. Many other organizations across India are following this spirit of seva, focusing on empowering communities while solving modern problems. For example, in rural areas, groups often train volunteers to provide basic healthcare services. These volunteers teach people about hygiene and disease prevention and help ensure that even the most remote areas have access to essential health services.

Education is another area where seva is making a difference. In rural and tribal regions, many organizations are working to bring education to children who might otherwise miss out. Volunteer teachers run informal schools that teach not only reading and writing but also life skills and practical knowledge. By focusing on education, these initiatives are helping to build stronger communities, as learning gives people the tools they need to improve their lives.

Beyond formal organizations, the idea of seva is also part of everyday life in India. People come together to help others during times of crisis, like after natural disasters, or to support marginalized groups. This spirit of helping one another is common in Indian culture and shows the importance of compassion and duty. People often help without expecting anything in return, and this quiet, selfless service strengthens the community.

What makes seva so powerful in India is that it focuses on empowering people, rather than creating dependency. The goal is to provide people with the skills and knowledge they need to improve their own lives. This approach leads to long-lasting change, as people are given the tools to become independent and contribute to their communities.

Even today, seva continues to play an important role in modern India. It mixes traditional values with new ideas, showing how the country can address today's challenges while staying true to its cultural heritage. By focusing on selfless service and empowering communities, India can create a better future for everyone.

Intergenerational Learning

Traditions are important because they connect generations, helping pass down wisdom, values, and culture from the past to the present. They allow each new generation to learn from the old and carry forward important practices, beliefs, and skills. This keeps the knowledge alive, ensuring it is not lost but adapted to fit modern times.

One good example of this is Indian classical music and dance. These art forms have been passed down through many generations, with families like the Gharanas in Hindustani classical music playing a key role in preserving and teaching them. A Gharana is a family tradition or style within classical music where the skills and knowledge are taught from one generation to the next. Through this, classical music is kept alive and continues to grow.

But Indian classical music and dance do not stay the same over time. They evolve and change, mixing with modern ideas to appeal to today's audience. Artists like Ravi Shankar and Zakir Hussain show how traditional music can blend with other styles. Ravi Shankar, a famous sitar player, brought Indian classical music to the world stage, playing with international musicians and adding Western music influences. Zakir Hussain, a master tabla player, followed in his footsteps, combining Indian rhythms with global sounds to create something new while still respecting the tradition.

These artists show that traditions can grow and adapt. They don't have to stay the same; they can blend old and new ideas to create something fresh, while still keeping their cultural meaning. In this way, Indian classical music and dance stay relevant and exciting for both old and new audiences.

This shows how traditions help us connect with the past but also allow for change. They are a link between generations, keeping culture alive while allowing it to grow and change over time.

Traditions as a Base for Innovation

Indian culture's natural adaptability is what makes it so fertile for new ideas. People are able to blend the old with the new, creating something that is both rooted in history and relevant to the present day. This openness to creativity and change has allowed India to remain dynamic and ever-evolving, while still preserving its rich cultural heritage. By combining tradition with a modern outlook, Indian society has found ways to innovate and thrive in the modern world, ensuring that its culture remains vibrant and relevant for future generations.

Sustainable Architecture Rooted in Tradition

Traditional Indian architecture has always been closely connected to the environment, with a deep understanding of natural elements such as sunlight, air, and temperature. The focus on creating buildings that harmonize with nature rather than overpower it has made Indian architecture a source of inspiration for modern green building practices. This approach has influenced the way architects and urban planners design structures today, particularly when it comes to sustainability and energy efficiency.

One of the key principles in traditional Indian architecture is the emphasis on natural ventilation. In many traditional Indian homes, large windows, open courtyards, and strategically placed vents allowed for natural airflow, keeping indoor spaces cool without the need for artificial air conditioning. This principle of passive cooling and ventilation is being revived today, especially in urban areas where buildings are designed to reduce energy consumption and make the most of the natural environment. By creating spaces that allow air to flow freely, buildings stay comfortable without relying heavily on energy-intensive systems, thus reducing their carbon footprint.

Sustainable materials have always been a key feature of Indian traditional architecture. Many older structures were built with locally sourced materials such as mud, stone, bamboo, and wood. These materials were not only environmentally friendly but also cost-effective. In many rural areas, homes were built with these materials because they were readily available and required minimal transportation, reducing the carbon footprint. Today, this tradition is being carried forward, with architects using eco-friendly materials like mud bricks, recycled wood, and natural fibers to build homes that are both affordable and sustainable.

A prime example of how traditional Indian architecture is influencing modern sustainable building design is Laurie Baker, an architect known as the "Gandhi of Architecture." Laurie Baker took traditional Indian design principles and adapted them to create cost-effective, eco-friendly homes. His designs focused on using locally sourced materials and emphasizing natural ventilation and light. He also incorporated the use of terracotta tiles, brickwork, and other materials that were suited to the local climate, helping reduce the need for energy-consuming artificial systems. Baker's designs were not just about being environmentally responsible but also about making homes more affordable for the average person, particularly in rural and semi-urban areas. His legacy continues to inspire modern architects and builders, especially those focused on sustainable, low-cost housing solutions.

Today, firms like Biome Environmental Solutions in Bengaluru are carrying forward Laurie Baker's legacy and integrating traditional architectural wisdom into their designs. Biome Environmental Solutions uses principles of passive design, relying on natural light, ventilation, and local materials to create sustainable urban spaces. Their designs focus on reducing the environmental impact of buildings while also ensuring that they are comfortable, affordable, and adaptable to the needs of modern life. These firms work on everything from residential homes to large-scale urban projects, always keeping in mind the need for sustainability and a minimal ecological footprint.

Modern architects are also looking back at ancient Indian architectural wisdom for inspiration in creating sustainable urban spaces. Traditional Indian buildings, such as step wells, havelis, and temples, were designed to work in harmony with the environment. They incorporated local climate considerations, used sustainable materials, and focused on creating efficient, comfortable living spaces. By reviving these practices in the context of modern urban planning, architects are finding ways to build green cities that are energy-efficient and environmentally friendly, even in dense, fast-growing urban areas.

In addition to passive cooling and sustainable materials, traditional Indian architecture also placed a strong emphasis on the layout and orientation of buildings to maximize natural resources like sunlight. The positioning of doors, windows, and courtyards was often done in such a way that the building could capture the sun's warmth in winter and stay cool in the summer. This passive approach to heating and cooling is now being revisited in modern designs, where architects are using similar principles to design energy-efficient buildings that require less reliance on artificial heating and cooling systems.

In conclusion, traditional Indian architecture offers a wealth of knowledge and practices that are proving to be incredibly relevant in the modern age of sustainable design. From using natural ventilation and eco-friendly materials to creating buildings that work in harmony with their surroundings, Indian architectural principles continue to inspire modern green buildings. Architects like Laurie Baker, along with firms like Biome Environmental Solutions, are blending these age-old ideas with modern technology and materials to create homes and cities that are not only sustainable but also comfortable, affordable, and energy-efficient. By drawing on the wisdom of the past, we can build a more sustainable and environmentally responsible future.

Narendra Modi's Campaigns on Tradition and Modernity

Prime Minister Narendra Modi has been instrumental in blending India's rich traditions with the demands of modernity, positioning India as a leader on the global stage. His leadership has highlighted how India's ancient culture, wisdom, and practices can coexist and even drive contemporary change. Through his initiatives and policies, he has shown that modern development and traditional values can go hand in hand, creating a bridge between the old and the new.

One of the clearest examples of this is Modi's promotion of yoga, which he has successfully linked to modern health and wellness trends while emphasizing its deep spiritual and cultural significance. By declaring the International Day of Yoga in 2014 and leading global efforts to celebrate it, Modi ensured that yoga, which is deeply rooted in India's spiritual practices, would be embraced worldwide. At the same time, he connected it to the growing global focus on physical and mental well-being, helping yoga transcend its spiritual origins to become a global health movement. This approach not only preserves the ancient tradition but also adapts it to the needs of modern society, making it relevant to millions of people across different cultures and backgrounds. Through this initiative, Modi effectively merged India's traditional spiritual practices with the global wellness trend, turning yoga into an international movement that emphasizes balance, health, and peace.

In addition to promoting yoga, Modi's Make in India campaign is another example of how he has merged India's traditional strengths with modern aspirations. India has a long history of craftsmanship and innovation, from its ancient textile industry to its historical contributions to mathematics, astronomy, and medicine. Modi's Make in India initiative draws on this history, encouraging both international and domestic companies to set up manufacturing operations in India. The campaign aims to not only make India a manufacturing hub but also revitalize traditional industries, such as handloom weaving, pottery, and metalwork, with modern tools and techniques. By encouraging industries to look to the past for inspiration and innovation, Modi has promoted a unique blend of tradition and modernity. The focus on sustainable practices and craftsmanship through the Make in India initiative also helps revive ancient Indian practices, while integrating them with modern production processes to make India a key player in the global economy.

Modi's promotion of Ayushman Bharat (the National Health Protection Scheme) is another example where India's traditional focus on holistic health care is being merged with modern health policies. India has a rich history of holistic healing systems, including Ayurveda, Unani, and Siddha, which emphasize balance in the body, mind, and spirit. While modern medicine continues to play a crucial role, Modi has advocated for integrating these traditional healing systems with modern healthcare to provide affordable, accessible, and comprehensive care to India's population. Ayushman Bharat represents a holistic approach to healthcare that considers not only the treatment of disease but also the prevention of illness through traditional methods, including nutrition and lifestyle changes that align with Indian heritage.

In the sphere of urban development, Modi's initiatives like Smart Cities Mission are designed to modernize India's infrastructure while preserving the country's traditional values. The focus is on creating sustainable, inclusive cities that integrate modern technologies such as IoT, renewable energy, and waste management with traditional principles of community living, water conservation, and the use of natural materials. These smart cities aim to bring modern amenities to urban areas while maintaining respect for traditional practices that have stood the test of time, such as conserving water through traditional methods like step wells and promoting green spaces in urban environments.

Furthermore, Modi's focus on Digital India highlights how technology and tradition can go hand in hand. The goal of Digital India is to transform India into a digitally empowered society, bridging the rural-urban divide and providing access to technology across the country. This initiative has facilitated the use of technology for rural empowerment, from digital payments in villages to online education platforms. The blend of digital technology with traditional practices like panchayats (village councils) and local governance systems has given rise to more efficient and accessible services while ensuring that traditional community structures remain relevant in today's world.

Modi's leadership also emphasizes the importance of Atmanirbhar Bharat (Self-Reliant India), which seeks to build a strong, independent India by encouraging local production and consumption, while still engaging with the global economy. This initiative calls for a fusion of traditional Indian industries and modern technology to foster growth in key sectors such as agriculture, manufacturing, and renewable energy. By focusing on self-reliance, Modi encourages the nation to value its traditions of craftsmanship, local knowledge, and self-sufficiency, while pushing forward with innovation and modern industry practices.

Through these initiatives, Prime Minister Modi has shown that it is possible to merge tradition with modernity, creating a future where India's rich heritage is a key driver of progress. His leadership reflects an understanding that the future does not have to be a break from the past, but rather a continuation of the values and practices that have made India unique throughout history. By promoting initiatives that respect India's traditions while embracing modernity, Modi has positioned India to thrive in a globalized world, ensuring that its cultural identity remains strong even as it advances into the future.

Sudha Murthy: A Modern-Day Philanthropist with Traditional Values

Sudha Murthy is an embodiment of how traditional values can harmonize with modern-day philanthropy, making her a modern-day philanthropist with deep-rooted traditional beliefs. As a writer, social worker, and the chairperson of Infosys Foundation, Sudha Murthy has dedicated her life to helping others, using her position to address critical social issues in India, such as poverty, education, healthcare, and rural development. Her work has earned her recognition both in India and abroad, and her unique approach to philanthropy is a blend of modern-day solutions and age-old Indian values of selflessness, compassion, and community service.

One of the defining features of Sudha Murthy's philanthropic work is her deep commitment to the traditional value of seva, or selfless service. She believes that giving back to society is not only an obligation but a way to live a meaningful life. Growing up in a modest family, she was taught by her parents that helping others should be a natural part of one's life. This lesson stayed with her and shaped her approach to philanthropy. She has often emphasized that her wealth and success should be used for the betterment of society, especially the underprivileged. Sudha Murthy's understanding of seva transcends mere charity; she believes in empowering people and providing them with opportunities to improve their own lives, particularly through education.

Her dedication to education is one of the most prominent examples of how she blends modern needs with traditional values. Through the Infosys Foundation, Sudha Murthy has contributed to building schools, libraries, and providing scholarships to children from rural and marginalized communities. She believes that education is the key to breaking the cycle of poverty, and this belief comes from her traditional Indian understanding of the importance of knowledge. In Indian culture, knowledge has always been highly revered, and Sudha Murthy's efforts reflect this deep respect for learning. She has helped thousands of children gain access to education and has worked toward improving the quality of education in rural areas, ensuring that children who would otherwise have limited opportunities are given a chance to build better futures.

Moreover, Sudha Murthy's philanthropic activities reflect the traditional Indian value of sharing, a concept that emphasizes giving without expecting anything in return. Whether it is in the form of donations or her efforts in driving community development, she has shown that philanthropy goes beyond financial assistance. She has often personally involved herself in many of the projects, working on the ground level to ensure their success. Her hands-on approach is rooted in traditional Indian values of humility and personal involvement, where true service comes from a genuine commitment to the well-being of others.

In addition to education, Sudha Murthy's philanthropic work has focused heavily on healthcare, a crucial aspect of community well-being. She has helped establish healthcare facilities in rural areas and provided support for the treatment of individuals who cannot afford expensive medical care. This focus on healthcare is in line with the Indian tradition of caring for others and ensuring that the most vulnerable members of society are not left behind. In traditional Indian communities, healthcare was often provided by local healers or temples, and while modern medical institutions have taken over these roles, the idea of caring for the sick and vulnerable remains deeply ingrained in Indian society. Sudha Murthy's work ensures that these traditional values continue to play a role in modern society.

Additionally, Sudha Murthy's approach to philanthropy is not solely limited to financial donations but also involves the importance of volunteering time and effort for a cause. This idea of seva through action is deeply embedded in Indian culture, where one is encouraged to contribute personally to the welfare of others. Through the Infosys Foundation, she encourages people from various walks of life to contribute to the betterment of society, thereby creating a culture of giving and active participation. By doing so, she brings together traditional values of volunteerism with modern-day organizational support, creating sustainable and impactful changes in communities.

Sudha Murthy's ability to merge modern-day philanthropy with traditional Indian values is also reflected in her personal life and writing. As a bestselling author, she writes stories that reflect the core values of kindness, empathy, and simplicity. Through her books, she not only entertains readers but also imparts wisdom based on age-old traditions, showcasing the richness of Indian culture. Her stories often revolve around human relationships, the importance of compassion, and the lessons learned from life's struggles—all of which resonate with traditional Indian teachings. Through her writing, Sudha Murthy has been able to connect the hearts of people to deeper values and instill a sense of community and responsibility in her readers.

Another aspect of her modern philanthropy is the way she uses technology to spread her message. While her methods are deeply rooted in tradition, Sudha Murthy has embraced modern tools like social media and digital platforms to connect with a larger audience. This combination of traditional wisdom with modern communication channels has allowed her to reach people across the globe, encouraging them to join the cause of social change and community development.

In conclusion, Sudha Murthy is a modern-day philanthropist who seamlessly merges traditional Indian values with contemporary approaches to social change. Her work reflects her belief in the power of selfless service, compassion, and community support, principles that are as relevant today as they were in ancient India. Through her contributions to education, healthcare, and rural development, she has demonstrated that one can be rooted in tradition while also driving meaningful progress in the modern world. Sudha Murthy's life and work inspire others to think beyond material wealth and focus on the greater good, emphasizing that true success lies in how we use our resources to uplift others and make a positive impact on society.

CHAPTER TEN

SUSTAINABILITY AND TRADITION

In the modern world, sustainability has become a global necessity, as the planet grapples with the effects of climate change, resource depletion, and environmental degradation. While technological advancements have provided solutions, there is also a growing realization that ancient traditions hold valuable lessons for sustainable living. India, with its rich cultural heritage, offers a treasure trove of practices and philosophies that promote harmony with nature. These traditions are not relics of the past but living examples of how human progress can coexist with ecological balance.

Traditional Practices and Their Relevance to Sustainable Living

Sustainable Agriculture: Lessons from the Past

Agriculture has been the backbone of India for centuries, and traditional farming methods focused on sustainability long before the term became popular. Techniques such as crop rotation, intercropping, and the use of natural fertilizers like cow dung and compost have been practiced in India for generations. These methods not only maintained soil fertility but also ensured ecological balance.

Case Study: Zero-Budget Natural Farming (ZBNF)
Pioneered by Padma Shri awardee Subhash Palekar, ZBNF draws inspiration from traditional Indian farming techniques. It eliminates chemical fertilizers and pesticides, reducing farming costs while improving soil health. States like Andhra Pradesh have adopted ZBNF on a large scale, with over 6 million farmers transitioning to this method as of 2022.

Example: The Sikkim Organic Model
Sikkim became the world's first fully organic state in 2016. The state government's focus on traditional agricultural practices led to a 20% increase in crop productivity, improved soil quality, and a reduction in health issues caused by chemical farming. Sikkim's success highlights the potential of merging traditional wisdom with modern policy.

Water Management: Ancient Wisdom in Modern Times

Water management has always been crucial in India, as the country has historically faced periods of water scarcity due to its diverse climates and seasonal variations. Ancient India developed many effective and sustainable methods to manage water resources. With the challenges of modern urbanization and climate change, India is once again looking back at these traditional practices to solve contemporary water issues. By combining ancient wisdom with modern technology, India is working to conserve water and ensure that future generations have access to this essential resource.

In ancient times, water was seen as sacred and vital for life, and many systems were put in place to manage it efficiently. One of the most well-known traditional methods of water management in India was the tank or kund system. In regions like Rajasthan and Tamil Nadu, communities built large tanks to collect rainwater during the monsoon. This stored water would then be used during dry months for drinking, irrigation, and other needs. The tank system was a community-based approach, allowing people to rely on locally stored water without depending solely on rivers or wells.

Another ancient water management structure was the stepwell (or baoli). These were multi-level wells with steps that led down to the water. Stepwells were particularly useful in dry areas, like Gujarat, where temperatures could reach extreme highs and water sources might dry up. By storing large amounts of water below ground, stepwells helped ensure a steady water supply even during droughts. These stepwells were also community spaces, where people gathered and interacted.

Rainwater harvesting is another ancient practice that India is reviving today. This method involved capturing rainwater from rooftops or other surfaces and storing it in tanks or pits. The goal was to recharge groundwater levels and make water available throughout the year. With water levels depleting across India, rainwater harvesting is gaining popularity again as a way to conserve water and meet modern needs.

The aharr-pynes system in Bihar is another example of traditional water management. This system used a network of small canals and ponds to collect rainwater and direct it to farmlands for irrigation. It helped farmers grow crops even during dry spells. Today, engineers and scientists are studying this system to see how it can be adapted to modern agriculture, especially as water scarcity continues to be a challenge.

In ancient India, water conservation was also part of religious and cultural practices. Many temples were built near water bodies like rivers and ponds. Pilgrims would bathe in these waters as part of their religious rituals, which helped keep these water bodies clean and maintained. Festivals like Pongal or Diwali also encouraged respect for water, with rituals that emphasized the importance of conserving it.

In recent years, the Indian government has recognized the importance of reviving traditional water management methods. In places like Rajasthan and Tamil Nadu, traditional practices such as rainwater harvesting and tank management are being promoted again. The Jal Shakti Abhiyan, a national campaign launched in 2019, encourages communities to restore old water systems like stepwells and ponds. This program aims to raise awareness about water conservation and help local communities take responsibility for their water resources.

Traditional water management practices are also being integrated with modern solutions. In cities, rainwater harvesting systems are being set up on rooftops, and waste water is being treated and reused. Modern technology is helping to improve traditional methods, making them more effective and adaptable to today's needs.

In conclusion, India's ancient water management systems offer valuable lessons in sustainability. By blending these traditional practices with modern technology, India is addressing current water issues and preparing for a more water-secure future. With the revival of methods like rainwater harvesting, tank management, and community-based approaches, India is working toward a solution that respects both its past and future needs. These ancient practices, combined with modern innovation, are crucial for managing water resources in a sustainable way.

Waste Management: Turning Back to Basics

Waste management in India, and across the world, is becoming an increasingly critical issue as urbanization grows and consumption patterns change. As modern cities expand, waste production also increases, leading to pollution, environmental degradation, and strain on waste management systems. While modern solutions to waste management are important, India is also turning back to its traditional methods, which were more sustainable and eco-friendly. The country's rich history offers valuable lessons in waste management, rooted in practices that focused on reducing waste, reusing resources, and living in harmony with nature.

In ancient India, waste management was handled by community-based practices that were simple but effective. Traditional Indian households, particularly in rural areas, practiced a circular economy by reusing and recycling materials. For example, food waste was commonly composted and used to enrich the soil for farming, while plastic, glass, and metal containers were reused until they could no longer serve their purpose. People did not rely heavily on disposable products and instead made use of biodegradable materials like bamboo, jute, and clay. These sustainable practices kept the environment clean while minimizing waste generation.

A key concept in traditional Indian practices is swachhata (cleanliness), which is deeply ingrained in cultural and religious practices. In Hinduism, for instance, cleanliness is considered not just a physical but also a spiritual activity. This idea extended to the management of waste. Household waste was sorted and disposed of in an organized manner, with different types of waste such as food scraps, ashes, and organic matter separated for composting. This careful attention to waste ensured that landfills were kept to a minimum and that materials were recycled in nature.

The traditional Indian practice of using clay pots, wooden utensils, and leaf plates also played a significant role in reducing waste. These items were biodegradable and could be disposed of without causing harm to the environment. In contrast, the rise of plastic and synthetic materials in modern times has made waste management more difficult. Plastic, in particular, is a significant pollutant, and traditional practices of using natural, reusable, and compostable materials are being revived to combat plastic waste.

Modern-day waste management systems in India are starting to integrate these traditional practices. One example of this is the growing interest in composting and organic waste management. Many urban areas are now promoting home composting, where households can recycle food scraps and yard waste into nutrient-rich compost that can be used for gardening or farming. This practice not only reduces the volume of waste but also decreases the need for chemical fertilizers, which are harmful to the environment.

Another important traditional practice that is being revived is the community-based waste management system. In rural India, waste management was often a collective responsibility, with local communities coming together to handle waste disposal, recycling, and composting. In cities, local organizations and citizen groups are beginning to follow this model by setting up community composting projects, waste segregation initiatives, and awareness campaigns about the importance of reducing waste. These grassroots movements encourage individuals to take responsibility for their waste, much like in the past, but with the added advantage of modern tools and technology to make the process more efficient.

One region in India where traditional methods of waste management are being revived is the state of Kerala. Kerala has been promoting the concept of sustainable waste management by encouraging residents to compost organic waste, segregate waste at the source, and recycle. Many localities have adopted this system with great success, drastically reducing the amount of waste that ends up in landfills. The state has also encouraged the use of eco-friendly alternatives, such as cloth bags instead of plastic, and the use of reusable containers in markets.

In addition to composting, traditional practices of waste minimization, such as reducing consumption and reusing materials, are gaining popularity in urban settings. For example, many cities now promote the use of cloth bags, reusable containers, and the reduction of single-use plastics. Schools and educational institutions are teaching students the importance of recycling, reusing, and reducing waste as part of environmental awareness programs.

The government of India has also been pushing for waste segregation at the source, an idea rooted in the traditional way of managing waste. By separating wet waste (organic) from dry waste (non-organic), much of the waste generated can be recycled or composted, reducing the burden on landfills and promoting a cleaner environment. In cities like Pune, waste segregation programs have been implemented successfully, with households and businesses sorting their waste into separate bins for collection.

In addition to reducing waste at the source, India is also exploring new technologies and methods to handle waste in an environmentally friendly way. One example is the use of waste-to-energy plants, which convert waste into electricity. While these methods are relatively new, they offer an innovative solution to waste management by turning waste into a resource. Additionally, waste recycling technologies that focus on reprocessing plastic, glass, and metal are being introduced to reduce the environmental impact of waste.

The key to effective waste management, however, lies in creating a mindset of responsibility toward the environment. It's important to recognize that modern waste management methods, while helpful, are not the sole solution. Reviving traditional practices and blending them with modern technology can create a more sustainable and effective approach to waste management. By reducing waste generation, reusing materials, and adopting sustainable practices, we can minimize our environmental footprint and contribute to a cleaner, greener planet.

Balancing Progress with Nature

India's rapid urbanization and industrialization pose challenges to its ecological balance. However, many individuals and communities are integrating traditional knowledge into modern development to create sustainable solutions.

Sustainable Architecture Inspired by Tradition

India's traditional architecture, from mud houses to forts, was designed to be energy-efficient and climate-responsive. These principles are now being incorporated into modern designs.

Example: *Laurie Baker – The Gandhi of Architecture*
Laurie Baker, an architect inspired by Mahatma Gandhi's principles, combined traditional Indian building techniques with modern needs. His low-cost, eco-friendly designs, using locally available materials like mud, bamboo, and stone, have influenced sustainable architecture across India.

Case Study: *Hunnarshala Foundation*
This Gujarat-based organization revives traditional building techniques like rammed earth and wattle-and-daub while training local artisans. Their approach combines sustainability with disaster resilience, as seen in their reconstruction efforts post the 2001 Gujarat earthquake.

Urban Sustainability: Ancient Practices in Modern Cities

Urban sustainability is a growing concern in modern cities as population growth, industrialization, and climate change put pressure on resources like water, energy, and space.

While modern cities focus on technological solutions to these problems, India is increasingly turning to its ancient practices for inspiration. These traditional methods, rooted in respect for nature and sustainability, offer valuable insights that can be adapted to today's urban challenges.

In ancient India, cities were built with a deep understanding of the environment. Traditional architecture, for example, often used natural materials like stone, clay, and wood, which were not only abundant but also eco-friendly. The design of homes and buildings focused on natural ventilation and lighting, reducing the need for artificial heating, cooling, and lighting. This approach helped keep energy consumption low, making cities more sustainable long before the modern concept of energy efficiency existed.

ancient practice that contributes to urban sustainability is the concept of *Jugaad*, or innovative problem-solving. In traditional Indian society, people often found creative, low-cost solutions to problems using limited resources. Today, this spirit of resourcefulness is being applied in cities to find sustainable solutions to issues like waste management, energy conservation, and transportation. For example, some urban communities are using low-cost solar panels to generate renewable energy, or they are promoting shared transportation like carpooling to reduce emissions.

Example: *Auroville – A Sustainable Model*
The township of Auroville in Tamil Nadu is a global experiment in sustainable living. Drawing from traditional water harvesting and organic farming practices, it has become a self-sustaining community with minimal environmental impact.

Green Infrastructure: Bengaluru's Revival of Lakes
Bengaluru, once known as the "City of Lakes," has suffered

from unplanned urbanization. Efforts by local activists to restore lakes like Kaikondrahalli and Puttenahalli, using traditional water management techniques, are reviving the city's water bodies and providing a lifeline for biodiversity.

The Role of Indian Philosophy in Sustainable Living

Indian traditions are deeply rooted in the philosophy of living in harmony with nature. Spiritual concepts such as Ahimsa (non-violence) and Aparigraha (non-possessiveness) promote sustainability by advocating for mindful consumption and respect for all forms of life.

The Gandhian Model of Simplicity

Mahatma Gandhi's philosophy of simple living and high thinking remains relevant in addressing today's environmental crises. His principles inspired initiatives like the Khadi movement, promoting sustainable, handmade textiles. Modern fashion in India is increasingly influenced by traditional crafts, blending heritage with sustainability. Brands like Fabindia and the Khadi and Village Industries Commission (KVIC) are at the forefront of this movement, drawing inspiration from age-old techniques such as handloom weaving, natural dyeing, and embroidery. By promoting these practices, they provide livelihoods to artisans and keep traditional skills alive while also addressing environmental concerns. The use of organic fabrics, hand-spun threads, and minimal waste processes reflects a commitment to eco-friendly practices. This fusion of tradition and modernity not only celebrates India's rich cultural heritage but also aligns with global trends in sustainable fashion.

Tribal Wisdom and Nature Conservation

India's tribal communities and individuals continue to exemplify sustainable living through their harmonious relationship with nature. The Bishnois of Rajasthan, with their centuries-old commitment to conserving wildlife and trees, remain iconic for their sacrifices during the 18th-century Khejarli Massacre. Similarly, the Warli tribe of Maharashtra incorporates ecological wisdom into their daily lives, using natural materials for their art and rituals. The Apatani tribe of Arunachal Pradesh practices sustainable farming by ingeniously integrating fish farming with wet rice cultivation, ensuring minimal environmental impact. Individuals like Tulsi Gowda, known as the "Encyclopedia of Forests," have planted and nurtured thousands of trees, passing on traditional knowledge about biodiversity. These examples underline the timeless wisdom of India's tribal communities in preserving the environment, offering valuable lessons for modern sustainable practices.

Sustainability in Education and Awareness

Education is key to connecting traditional knowledge with modern sustainability efforts, and many initiatives in India reflect this synergy. Schools in rural areas are teaching students traditional methods like rainwater harvesting, organic farming, and herbal medicine to preserve indigenous knowledge while addressing modern environmental challenges. The Chipko Movement, led by villagers in Uttarakhand, remains an inspiration for environmental education, demonstrating the power of grassroots efforts rooted in tradition. Youth-led organizations such as Fridays for Future India and Youth for Climate are blending activism with traditional Indian values like conservation and harmony with nature, promoting sustainable living. These efforts, supported by programs that integrate traditional crafts, biodiversity conservation, and eco-friendly innovations into curricula, are fostering a new generation that respects tradition while innovating for a sustainable future.

Statistics and the Path Forward

One of the most visible examples of India's leadership in sustainability is its focus on renewable energy. India is now the third-largest producer of renewable energy in the world and aims to reach 500 GW of non-fossil fuel energy capacity by 2030. Large solar parks, wind farms, and hydroelectric projects across the country contribute to reducing dependence on fossil fuels. Many of these projects are designed with traditional ecological practices in mind, such as minimizing land use and avoiding harm to local ecosystems. Solar energy, which is abundant in India, has been especially transformative, powering homes in rural areas and reducing carbon emissions in cities. These efforts not only showcase India's dedication to renewable energy but also highlight how modern solutions can draw inspiration from the sustainable practices of the past.

India's cultural tourism also plays an important role in promoting sustainability. States like Kerala have embraced eco-tourism, showcasing traditional lifestyles and practices that respect nature. Kerala's famous houseboats, for instance, now use solar power to reduce pollution while maintaining their cultural charm. Similarly, village-based tourism in states like Rajasthan and Gujarat allows visitors to experience traditional crafts, organic farming, and water conservation methods. These initiatives support local communities by providing income while also teaching visitors about sustainable living. Cultural tourism connects people to India's heritage and reminds them of the importance of living in harmony with the environment.

Individual efforts also play a significant role in India's journey toward sustainability. People like Jadav Payeng, known as the "Forest Man of India," and Tulsi Gowda, called the "Encyclopedia of Forests," have shown the power of personal dedication. Jadav Payeng created a 550-hectare forest on barren land in Assam over 40 years, while Tulsi Gowda has planted thousands of trees and shares her deep knowledge of plants and biodiversity. Their work reflects India's tradition of living in harmony with nature and inspires communities to take similar actions.

Sustainability is not just about large-scale projects or government policies; it is a way of life deeply embedded in Indian culture. Practices like composting, reusing materials, and minimizing waste were common in traditional Indian households and are now being encouraged in modern cities. For instance, many urban communities are adopting composting to manage organic waste and reduce the burden on landfills. These small but meaningful steps demonstrate how traditional values can shape everyday actions for a better future.

Reviving and Reinterpreting Traditions

India's traditions have withstood the test of time, evolving while retaining their essence. In today's globalized world, these traditions are not just surviving; they are being reinterpreted, reimagined, and revived to fit the aspirations of modern society. Whether through arts, crafts, cultural practices, or education, India is experiencing a cultural renaissance that blends the old with the new, ensuring that traditions remain relevant while meeting the demands of a rapidly changing world.

The Revival of Traditional Art Forms

Indian arts and crafts have always been an important part of the country's culture and history. Today, with the help of new ideas and technology, these traditional crafts are finding new ways to stay alive. They are being used in modern designs and products, making them popular again while still keeping their original charm. This mix of old and new shows how creative and adaptable Indian artisans are.

Warli paintings from Maharashtra are a great example of this change. These paintings were once made by tribal communities to show their daily lives. They used natural materials and painted on mud walls. Now, Warli designs are being used in home décor, clothes, and even digital art. Companies like Zola India work with local artists to create items like cushions, lamps, and tableware with Warli patterns. Thanks to technology, these designs are also being turned into digital formats, making them useful for graphic art, advertising, and modern art projects.

Phulkari embroidery from Punjab is another example. This colorful embroidery was traditionally made for weddings and special occasions. Today, Phulkari designs are being used in modern fashion. They appear on dresses, bags, and even shoes. Designers like Manish Malhotra and Anita Dongre have brought Phulkari to international runways, giving it a global audience. By using these patterns in modern styles, the tradition stays alive while also becoming more popular worldwide.

Similarly, the intricate block printing of Rajasthan has been given a modern touch. Known for its bold and vibrant patterns, this craft is now being used to create contemporary outfits and home textiles. Sustainable fashion brands are incorporating block printing techniques into their collections, appealing to environmentally conscious customers. Technology has also helped in creating more precise designs while maintaining the handmade feel.

Pattachitra paintings from Odisha, a centuries-old art form that tells stories of mythology, have found new life in products like handbags, sarees, and stationery. Artists are now working with designers to adapt these traditional patterns for everyday use, making them more relatable for younger generations.

Even pottery, a craft as old as civilization, is evolving. Terracotta pottery, for instance, is no longer just about traditional vases or lamps. Artisans are now creating contemporary designs like mugs, plates, and decorative pieces that suit modern homes. Online platforms have also made it easier for these artisans to reach customers worldwide.

Modern artists like Raja Ravi Varma in the past and contemporary creators such as Jiten Thukral and Sumir Tagra have played pivotal roles in blending traditional Indian motifs with modern storytelling. Their art represents how age-old techniques can find relevance in today's world.

By blending traditional skills with modern designs and technologies, Indian arts and crafts are not just surviving but thriving. They are connecting people to the country's rich heritage while adapting to new tastes and lifestyles. This transformation ensures that these crafts will continue to be a source of pride and inspiration for generations to come.

Global Demand for Indian Handicrafts

India's handicraft exports reached $4.35 billion in FY 2022-23, showing the world's growing appreciation for handcrafted, sustainable products. Initiatives like the "Vocal for Local" campaign have further boosted interest in traditional crafts. Platforms like Jaypore and iTokri connect artisans to global consumers, ensuring their work is valued and preserved.

The global demand for Indian handicrafts has been growing, driven by their unique designs, cultural richness, and the skill of Indian artisans. These handmade products, which reflect India's long history and traditions, are becoming more popular worldwide. As people look for authentic, sustainable, and eco-friendly products, Indian handicrafts are in high demand.

One reason for this growing interest is the variety of crafts from different regions of India. Each state has its own special crafts, such as the wood carvings from Kashmir, block prints from Rajasthan, silk weavings from Varanasi, and tribal art from Madhya Pradesh. This wide range of products attracts international customers who are looking for something unique and meaningful.

Another reason for the rise in demand is the global shift toward sustainable and ethical shopping. Many Indian handicrafts are made with eco-friendly materials, like natural dyes and recycled fabrics. These products are appealing to consumers who want to make responsible choices. Many companies also ensure that artisans are paid fairly, which makes these products even more attractive to buyers.

Technology and online shopping platforms have also played a big role in bringing Indian handicrafts to the world. Websites like Etsy, Amazon Handmade, and other platforms help small businesses and artisans sell their products internationally. Social media also allows artisans to showcase their work and connect with customers directly.

Indian handicrafts are also being adapted to suit modern trends. For example, traditional Rajasthani block prints are used in modern fashion, and Madhubani art is now found on items like cushion covers and wall hangings. Jewelry made using techniques like Kundan and Meenakari is loved worldwide for its beauty. Indian rugs and carpets, especially those from Kashmir, are also highly valued for their design and quality.

The Indian government has supported the growth of handicrafts by organizing trade fairs and providing help to artisans. Events like the India International Trade Fair and Surajkund Mela attract buyers from all over the world, helping Indian handicrafts reach a wider audience. Government programs like "Make in India" and "Skill India" also help artisans improve their products and compete in international markets.

Performing Arts: A Fusion of Classical and Contemporary

Reimagining Classical Dance

Indian classical dance forms like Bharatanatyam, Kathak, and Odissi have been brought back to life in new ways, thanks to creative performances that mix tradition with modern ideas. These dances, which have been part of India's culture for centuries, are now being updated to appeal to today's audiences around the world.

Rukmini Devi Arundale played a major role in bringing Bharatanatyam back to the stage in the early 20th century. She made this dance form more accessible by taking it from temples to public performances. Her work helped make Bharatanatyam popular again, and today, many dancers continue to adapt it by adding new themes, styles, and ideas while keeping its traditions alive.

Artists like Astad Deboo have also contributed to the evolution of Indian classical dance. Deboo mixed Bharatanatyam with modern dance styles, creating performances that are both traditional and contemporary. His work is known for combining storytelling with movement, and this fusion has helped bring Indian classical dance to international audiences, making it more relatable to people from different cultures.

Kathak, another classical dance form, has also evolved. Legendary dancers like Pandit Birju Maharaj have kept its traditional techniques but have also introduced new stories and music to make it more modern. Some Kathak dancers even mix the dance with other styles like jazz or ballet, creating performances that are fresh and exciting.

Odissi, a classical dance from Odisha, has also been updated by dancers who blend the traditional movements with new ideas. They use modern music, lighting, and stage designs, giving Odissi a new look while still honoring its ancient roots.

In all these dance forms, the combination of tradition and innovation has made Indian classical dance relevant and appealing to audiences around the world.

Music: Traditional Melodies with a Modern Twist

Indian classical music has always influenced music around the world, and this continues today. Artists like Ravi Shankar played a big role in introducing Indian instruments, especially the sitar, to Western countries. His collaboration with The Beatles helped bring Indian music to a global audience, inspiring many Western musicians to mix Indian sounds with their own music.

Today, fusion bands like The Raghu Dixit Project and Indian Ocean are continuing this trend by combining traditional Indian folk music with modern genres like rock. These bands have created a sound that appeals to younger audiences both in India and around the world. They mix Indian instruments and melodies with rock music, making Indian music more relatable to today's listeners while still staying connected to Indian culture.

What makes these bands special is how they blend the old and the new. For example, Raghu Dixit combines Kannada folk music with rock, using traditional instruments like the tabla and sitar alongside electric guitars. Indian Ocean mixes Indian classical and folk music with rock, jazz, and blues, creating a unique sound that is both Indian and global. These fusion bands are making Indian music more popular with modern audiences while keeping its cultural roots intact.

The Role of Technology in Reviving Tradition

One of the most significant ways the internet has helped preserve and promote Indian traditions is through websites dedicated to Indian crafts and culture. Websites like Craftsvilla and Indianculture.gov.in have made it easier for people, especially the younger generation, to access traditional knowledge and crafts.

Craftsvilla is an online marketplace that connects buyers with local artisans who specialize in handmade, traditional products. From clothing and jewelry to home décor, the website offers a wide range of products that showcase India's diverse craft traditions. What makes Craftsvilla special is that it brings these traditional crafts to a global audience. In the past, these crafts might have been limited to local markets or specific regions of India, but now anyone can buy and appreciate them.

Similarly, Indianculture.gov.in is an online platform that aims to promote India's rich cultural heritage. The website provides information on various aspects of Indian culture, including music, dance, art, literature, and handicrafts. It acts as an educational resource for anyone interested in learning about the history and significance of Indian traditions. With so much traditional knowledge available online, younger generations, who may not have had access to it through other means, can now easily connect with their heritage.

Social media platforms like Instagram, Facebook, and YouTube have become powerful tools for promoting traditional practices in a modern and appealing way. These platforms allow influencers and artists to share their work and inspire millions of people around the world. By using social media, influencers have been able to bridge the gap between traditional practices and modern trends, making them more relatable to younger audiences.

For example, Masaba Gupta, a popular fashion designer, has successfully blended traditional Indian prints with modern fashion. Masaba's designs incorporate vibrant Indian patterns and textiles, such as block prints and tie-dye, in contemporary clothing like dresses, skirts, and jackets. Her designs are not only fashionable but also celebrate India's rich textile traditions. Through her Instagram account, she showcases her designs and shares the story behind the fabrics she uses. This helps people understand the cultural significance of Indian prints while also making them trendy and appealing to a global audience.

Another influencer who has used social media to promote traditional Indian practices is Chef Ranveer Brar. Known for his love of Indian cuisine, Chef Brar uses his platforms to showcase the rich and diverse heritage of Indian food. Through his posts, videos, and cooking shows, he introduces traditional recipes from various regions of India, many of which are not commonly found in mainstream restaurants. Chef Brar's focus is not just on cooking but also on sharing the history and culture behind the dishes. He talks about the ingredients, cooking methods, and the stories behind each recipe, helping his audience connect with India's culinary traditions on a deeper level. His Instagram and YouTube channels have made Indian food more accessible to people all over the world, inspiring them to try cooking traditional dishes in their own kitchens.

Virtual Preservation of Heritage

Technological advances have made it easier to preserve and share India's rich cultural heritage. Through digital tools, many historical monuments, art forms, and artifacts that represent India's diverse history are being preserved for future generations. These efforts not only help protect heritage but also make it accessible to people around the world.

One of the most notable projects in this area is Google Arts & Culture's India Collection. This project allows users to explore India's historical sites, art, and culture virtually, from anywhere in the world. Google has partnered with several museums, cultural organizations, and heritage sites to bring India's history to a global audience. Through high-resolution images, 360-degree views, and interactive experiences, users can visit iconic monuments like the Taj Mahal, Qutub Minar, and temples of Khajuraho without leaving their homes. The project also features artwork, sculptures, and artifacts, showcasing India's rich artistic tradition. This digital collection helps not only preserve these sites but also educate people about India's cultural diversity and heritage.

Another significant effort in preserving India's heritage is the work being done by the INTACH (Indian National Trust for Art and Cultural Heritage) Heritage Academy. INTACH has embraced modern technology, such as 3D scanning and laser scanning, to document and restore heritage sites across the country. These tools allow for highly accurate digital records of monuments and heritage sites, creating 3D models that can be studied and analyzed without disturbing the physical structure. This technology is especially useful in preserving delicate structures that may be at risk of decay due to environmental factors or human activity.

The 3D scanning process works by capturing detailed measurements of a monument's surface, creating a digital replica that can be stored, analyzed, and even reconstructed. This helps experts to study the structure in great detail, plan restorations, and prevent further damage. It also allows for virtual tours, making these sites accessible to people who may not be able to visit in person.

In addition to documenting monuments, 3D scanning is also used for restoring artifacts. Through this technology, damaged or missing pieces of artifacts can be recreated digitally before being physically restored, ensuring that historical accuracy is maintained. This process of digital restoration helps preserve the authenticity of India's art and artifacts, ensuring that future generations can experience them in their original form.

Technological advancements in preservation and restoration are also opening doors for new research and education. With the help of digital platforms, scholars, historians, and students can access detailed data about Indian heritage, making it easier to study and understand the country's cultural legacy. For instance, virtual exhibitions allow global audiences to learn about India's art, history, and monuments in an interactive and engaging way.

These efforts to digitally preserve India's heritage are crucial for maintaining the country's cultural legacy in the modern world. By using technology, we can ensure that historical monuments, artifacts, and traditions are protected and shared with the world for generations to come.

Reinterpreting Traditions for Younger Generations

Indian education is increasingly blending traditional wisdom with modern knowledge. Schools like Rishi Valley School in Andhra Pradesh teach meditation and environmental sustainability alongside subjects like math and science, helping students connect with both their cultural roots and the modern world. Similarly, universities such as Nalanda University are being revived with a curriculum that merges ancient educational practices with contemporary learning, creating a unique educational experience. In parallel, Indian festivals like Diwali and Holi are being celebrated in eco-friendly ways, with initiatives like "Green Diwali" promoting organic colors, LED lights, and sustainable decorations. Social campaigns are also ensuring that the cultural significance of these festivals is preserved, while adapting them to address modern environmental concerns.

India's traditions are not static relics of the past; they are living, breathing entities that adapt to time and circumstance. By reinterpreting them for modern contexts, Indians are ensuring their survival while making them meaningful for the future. This chapter has explored how creativity, innovation, and technology are being used to keep traditions alive, showcasing the remarkable interplay of preservation and transformation.

Tradition and modernity, when harmonized, can open doors to new possibilities, offering not just a connection to the past but also a vision for the future. India, with its timeless wisdom and evolving spirit, continues to prove that the two can coexist, creating a legacy of resilience, creativity, and progress.

India – Past Forward

India's journey as a nation is not merely a story of progress and development; it is a reflection of the balance between preserving its age-old traditions and embracing modernity. This balance, often celebrated but occasionally misunderstood, is not a compromise but a deliberate choice—a model for growth rooted in values and vision. It speaks of resilience, adaptability, and a collective belief in creating a society that honors the past while shaping a future that is inclusive and forward-thinking.

As we reach the end of The India Story - Where Tradition Meets Transformation, I hope you've enjoyed exploring India's rich history, vibrant culture, and the fascinating ways in which its ancient traditions continue to shape and blend with the modern world. India's ability to balance its deep-rooted heritage with progress and innovation is a story of resilience, creativity, and wisdom.

Throughout the pages of this book, we have seen how India, with its diverse cultures, art forms, and values, has embraced change without losing sight of what makes it unique. From the revival of classical dance and music to the modern ways we celebrate our festivals, India's story is one of constant reinvention and adaptation. Even as we look towards the future, it is clear that our traditions remain the foundation of our strength and identity.

Looking ahead, India's future lies in its ability to redefine modernity on its own terms. True modernity is not about imitating the West but about creating a model of progress that reflects Indian values. It is about fostering innovation that uplifts communities, embracing diversity, and prioritizing sustainability. India's strength lies in its ability to adapt, to learn from the world while staying grounded in its heritage.

As India continues its journey, it offers a valuable lesson to the world: progress does not require abandoning the past. Instead, the past can be a source of inspiration and strength, a guide to navigating the complexities of the present and the uncertainties of the future. By honoring its traditions and embracing modernity, India is not only shaping its own destiny but also offering a blueprint for harmonious growth to the global community.

In this vision of India, tradition and modernity are not two separate paths but one intertwined journey. It is a journey of resilience, creativity, and hope—a journey that reflects the true essence of what it means to be Indian.

I hope this book has sparked a sense of pride and inspiration in you, as it has for me in writing it. India's journey is ongoing, and as we continue to move forward, we must honor both our past and our future. Thank you for joining me in this exploration of India's timeless story. I hope you had a good time reading it and that it has given you a deeper appreciation for the rich, ever-evolving story of our nation.

Gratitude

Thank you for taking the time to read *The India Story*. This book is not just a reflection of India's past and present, but also a celebration of the endless possibilities that lie ahead for this incredible nation. I've always believed that to understand where we're going, we must understand where we've come from. Through this book, I hope you've seen the richness of India's heritage and the brilliance of its people who continue to carry these traditions forward with pride and innovation.
I hope to see you all soon.
With gratitude and love,
Manasi Mehta